Educational System Planning

*PRENTICE-HALL EDUCATIONAL ADMINISTRATION
SERIES*
William Ammentorp, *Consulting Editor*

Educational
System
Planning

Roger A. Kaufman

United States International University

PRENTICE-HALL, INC., Englewood Cliffs, N.J.

© 1972 by PRENTICE-HALL, INC.
Englewood Cliffs, New Jersey

Library of Congress Catalog Card Number: 70–178159

ISBN: 0–13–237818–3

Printed in the United States of America

10 9 8 7 6 5 4

PRENTICE-HALL INTERNATIONAL, INC., London
PRENTICE HALL OF AUSTRALIA, PTY. LTD., Sydney
PRENTICE-HALL OF CANADA, LTD., Toronto
PRENTICE-HALL OF INDIA PRIVATE LIMITED, New Delhi
PRENTICE-HALL OF JAPAN, INC., Tokyo

To the critically important "Js" in my life

contents

preface

This work springs from many sources, only a few of which are reflected in the references. Formalization of the concepts of a useful system approach to education and the tools of mission analysis, function analysis, task analysis, and methods-means analysis perhaps first became possible from the funding and conduction of OPERATION PEP in California, an ESEA Title III project. As a result of this program, the author, Robert Corrigan, Betty Corrigan, and Donald Goodwin prepared training materials for OPERATION PEP participants.

Another federal grant paralleled and then continued this effort; under the Higher Education Act of 1965, Chapman College was given an Experienced Teacher Fellowship Program where we were able to develop and further expand earlier work done individually, as well as the concurrent OPERATION PEP activities. Much of both of these efforts is reflected in this book.

This work was improved by the critical and helpful suggestions of numerous California educators who were a part of these efforts and by the graduate students who worked with these ideas and formulations at Chapman College, the University of Southern California, and the United States International University.

As the notions received more exposure, the concepts were presented to concerned professionals in most states; and in a self-correcting manner, their responsible and constructive suggestions were incorporated into later formulations. And still today, as more and more people subject these ideas to critical examination and implementation in a world of children and adults, changes and modifications are resulting. The cycle will never be completed.

A great number of people have been helpful and inspirational to me in the frequently painful activities of developing the material for this book and for other previous formulations which serve as prologue. Bob Corrigan, Don Johnson, Leon Lessinger, Larry Belanger, Al Mayrhofer, JC Fikes, Jim Deese, Jim Finn, Les Shuck, Irene Cypher, Dick Hoffman, and Ted Blau come immediately to mind as being key in making me think more about things than I might have. The real credit, however, belongs to many, many professionals who have used and made relevant these few tentative and preliminary ideas. It is upon these many people that the credit for anything useful must be bestowed.

Acknowledgments

We would like to thank the following for permission to reprint material:

American Psychologist: R. A. Kaufman, "A Possible Integration Model for the Systematic and Measurable Improvement of Education," Vol. XXVI, No. 3, 1971. Copyright 1971 by the American Psychological Association.

AV Communication Review: R. A. Kaufman, "A System Approach to Education" (1968).

Educational Technology: R. A. Kaufman, "Accountability, A System Approach and the Quantitative Improvement of Education" (1971).

Utah System Approach to Individualized Learning (U-SAIL) funded under ESEA Title III.

Wasco Union School District: Mexican-American Research Project, "A Gestalt Approach to Developing the Bi-lingual, Bi-cultural Resources of the Mexican-American," under the Elementary and Secondary Education Act of 1965, Title III P.L. 89–10, Project number 68–5138, Grant number OEG 9–8–005138–0066 (056), United States Office of Education.

John Wiley & Sons, Inc.: S. S. Stevens, *Handbook of Experimental Psychology* (1962).

planning---an introduction

chapter 1

This is a book for educators about a process and a way of thinking that can help to create outcomes for education that dedicated professionals have sought for years. This process is designed to help achieve human dignity where it does not exist and to increase it where it only partially exists. It places each individual learner at the center and proceeds from the learner's point of entry. It is a precise way of assuring that the uniqueness and individuality of each person is formally brought to the forefront, there to serve as the basic referent for educational planning and achievement.

The key to educational success lies in people, and any process can only be as good as the people who use it. The hope is that educators will find these ideas useful and worthwhile.

Some Definitions

One of the most difficult aspects of dealing with a discipline that may be new—educational system planning, for example—is terminology. Frequently unfamiliar words may be dismissed as "jargon" and communication really cannot take place.

Each time a word or concept appears in this book, there is an attempt to define it operationally, in terms of how one creates it or how one might determine its existence or nonexistence. Precision is important, for often fellow educators use the same words with different meanings, and thus communication breaks down. In order to help avoid this, some definitions are given right at the beginning.

System: The sum total of parts working independently and working together to achieve required results or outcomes, based on needs.

For example, a school could be a system (if it had objectives), a school district could be a system, and an instructional program could also be a system. According to this particular definition, if an entity has purpose and organization, it can be a system. But what do we do to assure that a system is humane and responsive? A process called a system approach is suggested.

System approach: A process by which needs are identified, problems selected, requirements for problem solution are identified, solutions are chosen from alternatives, methods and means are obtained and implemented, results are evaluated, and required revisions to all or part of the system are made so that the needs are eliminated.

A system approach, as used here, is a type of logical problem-solving process which is applied to identifying and resolving important educational problems. It is central to educational system planning (which is perhaps better termed educational success planning), and we will be taking a much closer look at it in later chapters.

The intent of this volume is to introduce some tools and concepts and an associated way of thinking that are useful in identifying for resolution high-priority educational needs and problems in a more orderly, systematic, objective manner than most of us have previously employed.

A System Approach Is a Tool and a Way of Thinking

We have indicated that a system approach is both a process tool for more effectively and efficiently achieving required educational outcomes and a mode of thinking that emphasizes problem identification and problem resolution. It utilizes a formulation of logical problem-solving techniques that has become familiar and useful, particularly but not exclusively in the physical and behavioral sciences and in human communication. As science and scientific methodology are processes, so are planning and a system approach to education processes. The *outcomes* (or *products*) of the process depend on:

1. The validity of the data that are used to identify and resolve educational problems, and
2. The objectivity of the personnel using a system approach and its associated tools in planning.

A System Approach Should Make Education Humane

It is of critical importance to educational success that the individuality of each person be considered and preserved in the design and application of any functional educational process. Planning and the tools of a system approach focus on the learner and assure that each one's ambitions, capabilities, fears, hopes, and aspirations are considered and maintained.

It might at first seem a bit strange that precision and planning are humanizing, but it can be our best assurance that learners are not forced into arbitrary molds and categories, either by ignorance or by lack of appropriate tools for making education individually responsive. In his book *Future Shock*, Alvin Toffler (1970) makes the point well:

> *Arguing that planning imposes values on the future, the anti-planners overlook the fact that non-planning does so, too— often with far worse consequences.*

Not to plan at all, or not to plan on the basis of defining individual needs and characteristics is to chance the degradation of the person and his happiness, dignity, potential, and ability. A system approach, however, is only a process for identifying and resolving educational problems, and it can be only as functional and valid as the people using it allow and require. As L. E. Shuck states it, "Planning is just a substitute for good luck!" As a tool for change and problem solving, (problem solving as defined here is a process of going from a current condition to a required condition) a system approach can be useful to assure that change is humanely planned and valid.

The Anatomy of Change

As educators we can deal with change in several ways. We can be spectators to change, or we may be participants in it. All too often we are spectators and are swept along with conditions that cause us to constantly *react* to situational crises, or even to delay until others make decisions for us.

Most educational agencies today are involved in change. Students and teachers are becoming more organized in their demands for change, and many special-interest citizen groups exert pressure for and against educational programs and procedures. Changes are demanded of educators, frequently as if a single special topic or approach were the only critical element of an educational program.

It is common today to see educational codes growing bulkier and more intricate. Legislators are passing laws concerning educational practices and procedures at a rate that requires most educators to be speed readers, oracles, and magicians.

The social reformer is pressing for changes in curriculum, and an equal and opposite reaction comes from other groups wanting a change back to "the good old days." Wherever we are in education, there are pressures for us to be elsewhere.

If we simply *react* to demands for change, a type of anarchy tends to result in which we try to be everywhere at the same time and probably satisfy none of our clients (i.e., those whom we are attempting to serve).

Action, on the other hand, requires purpose, confidence, and results. When we *act* rather than *react*, we become accountable for both the educational processes and the educational products. The responsibility is ours; we make a professional commitment.

An action-oriented system approach to education requires that systematic and formal planning, design, implementation, evaluation, and revisions take place. There is a constant effort to achieve relevancy and practicality for the learners, so that they may survive and ideally contribute in society when they leave our educational agencies (Kaufman, Corrigan, and Johnson, 1969). Open, observable, and accountable, a system approach strives to identify priority needs and requirements and attempts to meet the needs efficiently and effectively. It allows for temporary failure in that it signals the requirement for revision when the system fails to meet the needs. The cliché that change is inevitable is still appropriate. The question for educators seems to be whether we will be the masters or the victims of change.

There is another aspect or characteristic of change which educators should consider—it seems to be threatening to virtually everyone. Beals (1968) states it well: ". . . the technological innovation which sooner or later arouses no resistance must be extremely trivial."

Change is apparently an extremely painful experience for most people. When an educator decides to change (or innovate), he must be prepared to meet resistance from many sources—his teachers, his administrators, his board, and even the members of his community. Since a system approach is a process for planned change, both the process itself and its outcomes will be questioned.

The threat from change is unfortunately a necessary price of relevancy. To remain static is to await decay and evolutionary extinction; to react is to risk dissipation of energy without achieving relevancy; and to innovate and act to increase our responsiveness to other people is to invite criticism. Planned change seems to be a professional responsibility, and it is suggested that a system approach will help provide the educator with the necessary tools and assurances that he will plan change well.

Action has greatest utility when valid data are used to predict practical and realistic results. A system approach, which is logical rather than emotional, is difficult to "sell" to some educators and citizens because many tend to operate on an emotional or "felt-need" basis. Yet progress has been made by the individual who, armed only with a valid requirement and a useful process, has set out and achieved an appropriate change. "Find a need and fill it" has been good advice that has been given to young citizens for some time. This approach to planning provides a process for finding the needs and the best way of meeting them.

Education is subject to change, and it is sensitive to change. New educational methods and techniques are always being introduced and tried, although not always on the most rational, empirical, measurement basis. In fact, educators often are accused of pursuing panaceas with nothing but hope and faith to guide them.

There seems to be a trend in many educational circles away from raw intuition and toward precision and placing the learner at the center of planning and doing (learner orientation). This shift is not in content of curriculum alone but also in design and implementation of curriculum.

Realistic Planning Starts with Identification of Outcomes

Planning best starts with the identification of needs. An educational need is defined as the measurable discrepancy (or gap) between current outcomes and desired or required outcomes. There are, perhaps, several ways of stating this gap, such as "the measurable discrepancy between 'what is' and 'what should be,'" or "the measurable gap between 'what is' and 'what is required.'" The important notion is that to have a need we must identify and document that there is a gap between two outcomes, that which is currently resulting and that which should be resulting. The setting of the two polar dimensions of a need should be done in a formal way, and such a procedure is called "needs assessment." Needs assessment is covered in some detail in Chapter 3.

In defining needs as gaps between two outcomes, it is important not to include in the statement of need any solution, or how-to-do-it, for getting from one to the other. Including a solution in a statement of need automatically reduces the options for meeting a need, and thus there is a possible reduction in the probability of finding new, innovative, or creative ways of bridging the gap. Also, when one includes a solution in a statement of need, there is a risk of jumping from unwarranted assumptions to foregone conclusions, for choosing a solution before the problem has been identified and selected might leave us unresponsive to the real concerns and gaps which exist in our educational world.

A needs assessment provides data for identifying and subsequently eliminating high-priority needs in our world of concern. Needs, when documented, provide the basic information for setting valid goals to better assure us that our educational "product" is relevant.

By identifying required outcomes (products) first, and then deciding about the most effective and efficient "process," we forestall the likelihood of having solutions that do not meet the actual needs. Since planning provides a method for identifying such needs and goals, it allows us to decide on a "map" of action (or accomplishment blueprint) to guide our efforts and our money toward relevant success.

It is not unusual to hear citizens and educators alike protest "we already know what our problems are, what we 'need' are solutions." This, most frequently, is not an accurate perception on their part. Usually, we know some symptoms of problems, but frequently we do not know the exact nature of the problem.

If we attempt to solve problems poorly defined, we are faced with (1) an infinite number of possible solutions, and/or (2) a situation in which we treat only the symptoms and never really solve the problems. The analogy would be a physician who prescribed aspirin for a patient with a headache, only to find out later that the patient had a brain tumor. It is important not to confuse means and ends, but to realize the important distinction and relations between products (outcomes) and process (ways of achieving outcomes)!

Planning, and the commitment to planning before taking action, can prevent us educators from putting the cart before the horse by deciding how we are going to do something before we know what should be done. It will also keep us from merely treating symptoms (with marginal success or perhaps even failure).

What is planning? A plan is a projection of what is to be accomplished to reach valid and valued goals. It includes the elements of:

Identifying and documenting needs.

Selecting among the documented needs those of sufficient priority for action.

Detailed specification of outcomes or accomplishments to be achieved for each selected need.

Identification of requirements for meeting each selected need, including specifications for eliminating the need by problem solving.

A sequence of outcomes required to meet the identified needs.

Identification of possible alternative strategies and tools for accomplishing each requirement for meeting each need, including a listing of the advantages and disadvantages of each set of strategies and tools (or methods and means).

Planning, then, is only concerned with determining *what* is to be done so that practical implementing decisions may be made later. Planning comes before doing. Planning is a process for determining "where to go" and identifying the requirements for getting there in the most effective and efficient manner possible.

Education—A Management Process

Education occurs in a context of values (Rucker, 1969a)—what do the various partners of education require and expect? Usually, the public sectors associated with education provide funds and resources for educators to achieve that which they value. Regardless of whether the requirements are well defined, the public still holds educators responsible for outcomes and for the utilization of resources. Education has its expression through a series of products (or outcomes) which the process is expected to achieve.

The educational process may be managed, mismanaged, or fall into categories between these extremes. An overall educational management process model (Kaufman, 1968, 1969, 1970; Corrigan, 1969) may be conceived as being constituted of the following elements:

1. Identify problem (based upon documented needs).

2. Determine solution requirements and solution alternatives.

3. Select solution strategies (from among the alternatives).

4. Implement selected strategies (to achieve the required outcomes).

5. Determine performance effectiveness.

6. Revise as required at any step in the process.

The foregoing is (or should be) a continuous process, and actually consists of the subelements of (1) *problem identification* and (2) *problem resolution.* Problem identification is the primary concern of steps 1 and 2 and problem resolution is the concern of steps 3, 4, and 5 of educational management. The sixth step is used in both problem identification and problem resolution. This process for educational management is also called a system approach.

Simply, any time educational change is to occur, the process just described is viable. It is a closed-loop or self-correcting process—when requirements are not met at any time during the process, the appropriate revisions are demanded. Therefore, at each step there is a requirement to determine whether the plan has succeeded and to make decisions regarding continuation or revision. In planning we must identify all elements and requirements for achieving valid change utilizing the suggested six-step management process.

The major focus of this book is on problem identification, and the tools, procedures, and logic of needs assessment and system analysis. The "doing" aspects of a complete system approach (system synthesis) are briefly described and only related to planning. The emphasis here, then, is determining what to do, and mastering the tools of responsible planning. Armed with these skills, and with the aid of a number of good references in this area, the reader may plan the necessary "doing" (or synthesis) aspects of a system approach.

Summary

A system approach to education, as a problem-solving process, seems to fit the requirements of educators who want relevant and predictable learner-oriented results. The relation between product and process (or ends and means) has to be placed into perspective by a planning tool and an associated logic calling for the identification of needs and their associated problems *before* solutions are identified and selected.

The self-correcting nature of a system approach better assures an objective basis for learning and learning management. Educators are becoming more logical and analytical, and a system approach is being evolved as a useful process tool.

The process described here will provide the educator who intends to make useful, systematic, organized change with the necessary information for achieving new educational success; additionally it will supply him with a realistic rationale for any such change. This process does not automatically assume that everything now going on is bad, nor does it assume that everything is useful or that every proposed change is potentially good! It intends to maintain that which is worthwhile and useful, and also to identify areas in which new and more successful ways and means can help us reach every learner, and, as suggested by Lessinger (1970), make "every kid a winner."

Glossary

Need (educational): the measurable discrepancy between "where we are now" and "where we should be," in terms of outcomes, or results.

Needs assessment: the formal process for identifying outcome discrepancies.

Plan: a projection of what is to be accomplished to reach valid and valued goals.

Process: the application of the ways and means for achieving any result, or outcome.

Product: the result, or end, or outcome.

System: the sum total of parts working independently and working together to achieve required results or outcomes, based upon needs.

System approach: a process by which needs are identified, problems are selected, requirements for problem solution are identified, solutions are selected from alternatives, methods and means are obtained and implemented, results are evaluated, and required revisions to all or part of the system are made so that the needs are eliminated.

Exercises[1]

1. The definition for planning used in this book is ＿＿＿＿＿＿＿＿ ＿＿＿＿＿＿＿＿＿＿＿＿＿＿＿＿＿＿＿.

2. A system approach, as used in this book, is defined as ＿＿＿＿＿＿ ＿＿＿＿＿＿＿＿＿＿＿＿＿＿＿＿＿＿＿＿＿＿＿＿＿＿＿ ＿＿＿＿＿＿＿＿＿＿＿＿＿＿＿＿. (use your own words—remember that these are concepts, not fodder for blind memorization.)

3. A system approach is (choose one): (a) a panacea, (b) a process tool, (c) a method based on computer technology, (d) a process for planning and doing.

4. Discuss, either pro or con, the following: "If used properly, a system approach to education can make education more humane."

5. Realistic planning starts with an identification of ＿＿＿＿＿＿.

6. What is planning?

7. What is the relation between means and ends?

8. Give the six elements of an overall management process as defined here:

    a. ＿＿＿＿＿＿＿＿＿＿＿＿＿＿＿＿＿＿＿＿＿＿＿＿＿＿＿
    b. ＿＿＿＿＿＿＿＿＿＿＿＿＿＿＿＿＿＿＿＿＿＿＿＿＿＿＿
    c. ＿＿＿＿＿＿＿＿＿＿＿＿＿＿＿＿＿＿＿＿＿＿＿＿＿＿＿
    d. ＿＿＿＿＿＿＿＿＿＿＿＿＿＿＿＿＿＿＿＿＿＿＿＿＿＿＿
    e. ＿＿＿＿＿＿＿＿＿＿＿＿＿＿＿＿＿＿＿＿＿＿＿＿＿＿＿
    f. ＿＿＿＿＿＿＿＿＿＿＿＿＿＿＿＿＿＿＿＿＿＿＿＿＿＿＿

9. Define an educational need: ＿＿＿＿＿＿＿＿＿＿＿＿＿＿＿＿＿＿ ＿＿＿＿＿＿＿＿＿＿＿＿＿＿＿＿.

---

1. *Each chapter presents exercises intended to serve as the objectives for the chapter and provide a review of important concepts.*

education as a management process- an introduction to a system approach to education

chapter 2

The material in this chapter is intended to give you an "over-view" of the tools for planning and their relation to the process we have already called a "system approach" to education. The tools for educational planning include needs assessment and system analysis. Needs assessment is a type of discrepancy analysis which helps to tell us where we are now and where we should be going. System analysis builds from that base, and identifies the requirements for whatever action is indicated. The exact nature of each step and its associated tool, how the tool works, and what it is good for, may not become altogether clear until each tool has been explained (see following chapters); but this brief introduction should furnish an overall picture of the tools for educational system planning.

Education itself may be viewed as a process for providing learners with (at least minimal) skills, knowledge, and attitudes so that they may live and produce in our society when they legally exit from our educational agencies. The "product" of education is no less than the achievement of these required minimal skills, knowledges, and attitudes. The behavior and achievements of learners as they function as citizens determines whether the "product" has been achieved.

It would seem useful to conceive of the educator—an administrator, a counselor, a teacher, a planner, or a curriculum specialist—as a *manager* of the learning process. The management of learning involves ascertaining learner needs, identification of problems, and then the application of a process or a number of procedures to fashion an educational system responsive to the identified needs and requirements. The product of this management process, then, is identical to the product of education: the required skills, knowledge, and attitudes of learners.

Management and Accountability

The job of an educational manager is to plan, design, and implement an efficient and effective learning system, responsive to the needs of the learner and of society. Successful management requires, as Lessinger (1970a) points out, an accountability for the outcomes of the system. Outcomes are specified in measurable performance terms, and achievement of these outcomes is openly determined so that required revision and redesign may take place. Of course the educational agencies of our nation cannot be completely responsible for all the behavior of all the children, but they are usually charged with the responsibility of educating the young. Interacting variables of the home, the neighborhood, the culture, and the society must be accounted for in educational design, for regardless of our pleas we are still held accountable. When we try to avoid this accountability, other agencies are either selected or created to perform educational functions.

Since the educator of today is considered to be accountable for his efforts, he must state his goals, objectives, and procedures openly. He must begin to speak to taxpayers and legislators in terms of learning outcomes such as reading ability and occupational skills, rather than talking only about *processes* for education such as differentiated staffing and programmed instruction. The outcomes of educational efforts are becoming a matter of public record and public concern. The processes and tools for education should be selected by the professional educator only after the partners in education—the citizens who pay the bills, the learners, and the professional educator—have agreed on what should be done, why, and to what extent.

Management of education may be viewed as the process for the achievement of required outcomes. Cook (1968b), for example, identifies two overall management functions: a planning subsystem and a control subsystem. MacDonald (1969) indicates that a five-part process of educational management aimed at reaching predefined objectives would include: planning, organization, staffing, direction, and control.

The management of education is defined here as a six-step process that includes:

1. Identification of priority needs and associated problems.

2. Determining requirements to solve the problem and identify possible solution alternatives for meeting the specified needs.

3. Selecting solution strategies and tools from alternatives.

4. Implementing solution strategies, including the management and control of the selected strategies and tools.

5. Evaluation of performance effectiveness based on the needs and the requirements identified previously.

6. Revision of any or all previous steps (at any time in the process) to assure that the educational system is responsive, effective, and efficient.

These six steps, which may be considered a problem-solving process, form the basic process model for a system approach to education. This process model, or related variations, have been delineated by Corrigan and Kaufman (1965, 1966, 1967, 1968), Lehmann (1968), and Carter (1969). It is a process for designing an overall educational system to achieve required outcomes based on needs.

Kaufman (1968) summarizes work conducted over a number of years with Corrigan by attempting to define such a system approach in terms of a generic problem-solving process. Using an example of solving a problem such as $X + 1 = 10$, a six-step process model was demonstrated which was a self-correcting process for identifying and solving problems. Other examples of this derivation could be used (see, for example, Fig. 2.1 in

SITUTATION: A young child asks you to put together a picture (jigsaw) puzzle.

NEED: The puzzle parts are in disorganized array in a box and they are to be in an organized array.

PROBLEM SOLVING STEPS	PROCESS EXAMPLE
1. Identify problem (based upon need)	1. Assemble jigsaw puzzle
2. Determine solution requirements and solution alternatives	2. Requirements: A. Puzzle to be assembled by you B. Puzzle must be assembled in view of the child C. Puzzle must be assembled "quickly" (within 20 minutes) Alternatives: A. Tell child you do not have time B. "Trial and error" matching of parts C. Match parts by contours D. Match parts by colors E. Match parts by color and contours
3. Select solution strategy from alternatives	3. Select alternative "C"
4. Implement selected strategy	4. Lay out parts and match two or more parts by contours
5. Determine performance effectiveness	5. Check outcome against criteria stated in Step 2: Requirement Accomplished? A. YES B. YES C. NO
6. Re-do as required	6. If one or more requirement is not met, re-do any or all previous steps. (for instance, try alternative "D".)

FIG. 2.1. **An example of a generic (general) problem-solving process. After Kaufman (1970a).**

which assembling a jigsaw puzzle is subjected to this treatment). Success-ful management of education is possible with the use of such a system approach. It requires that interacting variables be formally considered in design and that outcomes be evaluated and necessary revisions made on the basis of performance. It is a planning, implementation, and control process requiring that the dynamics of educational management be con-ducted on a logical and orderly basis which can be evaluated, and that the accountable agent is the educator and his educational system.

A Description of a System Approach as a Design Process

If it is true that educational management may be conceived of as a problem-solving process that includes planning, design, implementation, control, evaluation, and revision, then a system approach seen as a design process may be a truly useful tool of educational managers/administrators (Kaufman, 1970b). Thus teachers become learning managers; adminis-trators become educational managers.

Following is a brief discussion of the basic six steps of such a man-agement process model; the six steps are grouped into two units: problem identification and problem resolution.

Problem Identification

Step 1—identify problems from documented needs: Earlier, educa-tional needs were defined as measurable discrepancies between a current situation and a required or desired situation. An example of such a need (strictly hypothetical) might be:

> *Learners in the Egge School District have a mean reading score*
> *of 32nd percentile and a standard deviation of 7 on the Utopian*
> *Valid Test of Reading Achievement. The district school board has*
> *required that the learners perform at the 50th percentile or better*
> *with a standard deviation not to exceed 5 on the Utopian Valid*
> *Test of Reading Achievement before June 13.*

This example shows a measurable discrepancy between "what is" and "what should be," namely, of a mean score difference of 18 and a standard deviation of 2. This stating of needs in measurable performance terms [such as suggested by Mager (1961), Popham (1966), and/or Smith (1964)] is a critically important feature of a system approach, since it provides a tangible, quantified starting referent for the design of a responsive educational system. A statement of need describes outcome gaps and therefore must be free of any solutions or "how-to-do-its."

Educational management using a system approach starts with an assessment of educational needs. The importance of starting system design from documentable needs cannot be overemphasized—it prevents the selection of solutions before the identification and specification of problems. (Needs assessment is discussed in detail in Chapter 3.) Thus the first step of an educational management process called a system approach is to identify problems based on documented needs. These problems should be stated in measurable, performance terms.

Step 2—determine solution requirements and solution alternatives: The needs assessment process has identified discrepancies for resolution on the basis of priority and has provided overall requirements for an educational system. These overall requirements serve as the "mission objective and performance requirements" for system design. By comparing this statement of the problem with the situations and outcomes currently experienced, the system planner can find out where he is going and how to tell when he has arrived.

Having used the statement of needs to describe both the current situation and the success they seek, the educational manager and the educational system planner must decide on the requirements to solve the problems they face. Using educational "system analysis," one can determine system requirements and *possible* solution strategies and tools in layers or levels of details from the most general to the most specific.

This management step does not select *how* to solve the problem(s), but rather determines *what is to be done and what alternative strategies and tools are available to accomplish each requirement.* Selection of the "hows" occurs in the next system approach step.

The tools of educational system analysis include:

1. Mission analysis.
2. Function analysis.
3. Task analysis.
4. Methods–means analysis.

These tools, described in greater detail in Chapters 4 through 7, form a process of determining requirements for educational system design and their feasibility, as well.

The system analysis process, a key tool used in this problem-solving process, is designed to determine the feasible "whats" for system planning and design by analyzing requirements and identifying possible alternatives in successive levels of increasing detail.

Let's take a closer look at these tools for system analysis, for each contribute a little more to the determination of (1) what is required to meet the identified need (gap), (2) what alternatives are available to achieve each requirement, and (3) what the advantages and disadvantages are of each alternative solution possibility.

First, the tools for determining the requirements for getting from where we are to where we should be are mission analysis, function analysis, and task analysis. All three help us to ascertain what is to be done to meet the need, but not how. The mission analysis tells us about requirements for the total problem, function analysis tells about more detailed aspects of each part of the total problem, and finally, task analysis breaks the problem down into the smallest units we will require for planning. The use of these three tools has been likened to looking through a microscope with several lenses of increasing magnification (Corrigan and Kaufman, 1966). The first lens (mission analysis) gives us the big picture, the second lens (function analysis) shows us a smaller part of the total problem in greater detail, and finally, the last lens we use (task analysis) gives us the exact detail of every part we saw in function analysis.

After we have identified all the parts of this system, we can identify possible methods and means (or strategies and tools) for each of the requirements we have unearthed during mission, function, and finally, task analysis—we match requirements against possible solutions and note the relative advantages and disadvantages of each so that we can later pick the best ones for solving our problem.

As we look at the individual tools presented in this chapter, and as we see them again in greater detail in the following chapters, think of them as peeling back layers of an onion—we go deeper and deeper into the "heart" as we go, and find out more about how the whole is put together.

Mission analysis:[1] Proceeding from the needs assessment and problems delineation, the mission analysis states the overall goals and measurable performance requirements (criteria) for the achievement of system outcomes. These required outcome specifications are closely related to the previously identified needs. The mission objective and its associated performance requirements state the appropriate specifications for the system being planned and designed.

Since, as we know, an educational system design procedure must take the planner from where he is to where he is to be, the next part of mission analysis is the statement of a management plan (called a mission profile) showing the "major" milestones or the central pathway for solving a given problem. An example of such a management plan, a possible

---

1. *Presented in detail in Chapter 4.*

mission profile for preparing instructional materials (if the mission is *just* that), is presented in Fig. 2.2.

It is interesting to note that the overall process model for a system approach may also be shown as a mission profile. Such a profile, containing a management plan for identifying and solving problems in a logical, orderly manner (or system approach), may be reviewed in Fig. 2.3.

"Flow charts" like those in Figs. 2.2 and 2.3 provide a tool for displaying (or describing) a system and its components and subsystem relationships in a simple, "at-a-glance" format. A flow chart, which identifies

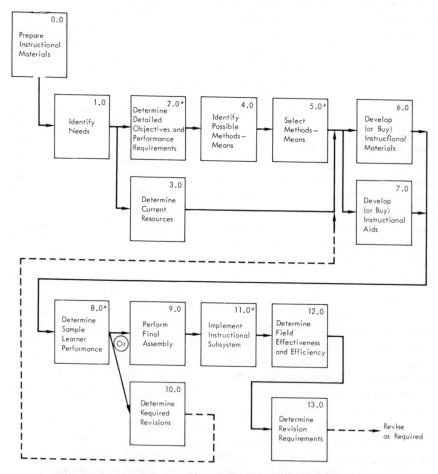

FIG. 2.2. A possible mission profile for preparing instructional materials using a system approach. All functions could interact with all other functions, so not all "feedback" or revision pathways are identified. An asterisk indicates a possible point for obtaining approval before proceeding. Based on Kaufman (1968, 1970a, b).

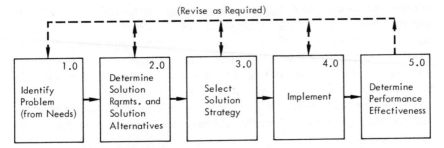

FIG. 2.3.   A general problem-solving process. Five of the six steps are identified and numbered; the last (revise as required) is indicated by the broken lines. Note that revision may take place at any problem-solving step. Based on Kaufman (1968, 1970a, b).

functions (or things to be accomplished) and their interrelations, may be read by following the solid lines and connecting arrows and by noting the order of the numbers. (Details of flow chart construction and interpretation are presented in Chapter 5.)

Mission analysis, then, is the system analysis step that tells (1) what is to be achieved (2) what criteria will be used to determine success, and (3) what are the steps (functions) required to move one from the current situation to the desired state of affairs. The steps and tools of mission analysis are:

Functions	*Tools*
1. What is the system to accomplish and what criteria will be used to determine success?	*1.* Mission objective and performance requirements.
2. What are the basic steps or milestones required to get one from where one is to where he should be?	*2.* Mission profile.

Function analysis:[2]   The mission profile has provided the basic functions, or milestones, that delineate the major "things" that must be performed. The next part of an educational system analysis is to identify and define *what* is to be done to get each one of the milestones in the mission profile accomplished.

Function analysis is the process for determining requirements and subfunctions for accomplishing each element in the mission profile. As such, it may be considered a vertical expansion of the mission profile.

Again, as was true for the mission objectives, each function in the mission profile will have performance requirements, and a "miniature"

2. *Presented in detail in Chapter 5.*

mission profile may be constructed to describe the functions that will get one from where he is to the accomplishment of each mission profile function. This increasingly detailed analysis of functions and subfunctions is illustrated in Figure 2.4, which depicts a hypothetical function analysis of a mission profile function of "identify problem . . . ," the first function in the generic system approach process model.

Note that each level of a function analysis carries a number identifying the level of analysis; function analysis, furthermore, may consist of several levels.

Task analysis: Task analysis is the arbitrary end-point of the analysis of "what is to be done" in a system analysis. It differs from mission and function analysis only in degree, not in kind.

The vertical expansion, or analysis, is continued through the function level until "units of performance" are identified (rather than collections of things to be done which are, again arbitrarily, called "functions"). The identification of tasks[3] and their ordering is the last "breaking-down" step of an educational system analysis.

Methods–means analysis:[4]   Recalling that an educational system analysis is a tool for determining feasible "whats" for problem solution and that the second step in a system approach to education is "Determine Solution Requirements and Solution Alternatives," let us look at the remaining step of a system analysis—the identification of possible methods and means (or strategies and tools) for achieving each of the performance requirements or group of performance requirements.

The methods–means analysis may be conducted after mission, function, and task analyses have been completed, or it may be conducted in parallel with each of them as the analysis of additional requirements progresses from level to level. Fig. 2.5 shows a "process diagram" for conducting a methods–means analysis in such a parallel (or on-going) fashion.

A methods–means analysis identifies possible strategies and tools available for achieving each performance requirement or family of performance requirements and additionally lists the relative advantages and disadvantages of each for later selection in the next system approach step.

Methods–means analysis, like the other educational system analysis steps, determines *what* is to be done (what possibilities exist in the case of methods–means analysis) and not *how* it is to be accomplished.

3.   *Task analysis is presented in detail in Chapter 6.*
4.   *Presented in detail in Chapter 7.*

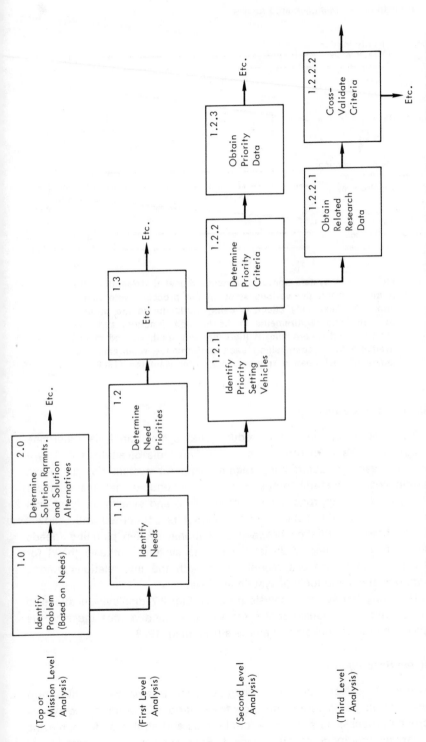

FIG. 2.4 An example of a hypothetical function analysis showing the manner in which any function may be analyzed into lower level constituent functions. Note that this is only a partial analysis and that each level is incomplete as indicated by "etc." Also each function shown may be analyzed into lower level functions. Based on Kaufman (1968, 1970a, b).

19

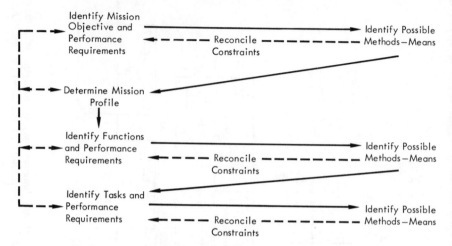

FIG. 2.5.   A system approach process model that identifies the relation among the various steps in the process. Note that a continuing feasibility check is being made during the process by identifying requirements in the mission, function, and task analyses and determining if there are any methods and means available for accomplishing each performance requirement or family of performance requirements. After Kaufman (1968).

System Analysis Summary

The steps and tools of an educational system analysis determine the feasible "whats" of problem solution. The tools of analysis and synthesis are used in determining requirements for system design. Again referring to the generic process model for educational management utilizing a system approach, needs assessment and system analysis deal with "what," and the balance of the model is concerned with "how." Fig. 2.6 shows the relation between educational system planning (needs assessment and system analysis) [what] and system synthesis [how] for the overall design-process model, along with the interrelations among the various steps and tools of system analysis.

Restating the system analysis process, Fig. 2.7 displays questions to be answered in an educational system analysis and relates these to the steps of an educational system analysis (Kaufman, 1968).

Problem Resolution

Step 3—select solution strategies from alternatives: This third problem-solving step begins the "how-to-get-it-done" portion of the system approach process. Here the appropriate tools and strategies for achieving the various requirements are selected. Frequently a choice criterion of

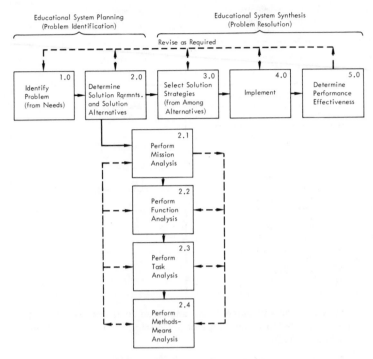

FIG. 2.6. A flow chart showing the "educational system planning" and "educational system synthesis" phases of a system approach and the steps of an educational system analysis. Note that the methods–means analysis, as shown, could be accomplished after completing mission, function, and task analyses *or* in parallel with each system analysis step. After Kaufman (1968, 1970*a*, *b*).

"cost-benefit" is used, that is, the selection from among alternatives that which will at least achieve the minimal requirements at the lowest cost. All too frequently, educators begin the system design procedure at this point—without the specific delineation of problems and requirements—and select the alternative methods and means on the basis of professional judgment or on a mere assumption of the problems and the requirements.

Selecting methods and means from alternatives requires that the various identified functions and tasks be allocated to (1) people, (2) equipment, and/or (3) people and equipment in combination.

Selection must be made on the basis of the system as a whole, noting the interactional characteristics of the various requirements of the system. Frequently tools of modeling and simulation are utilized to determine the most effective and efficient means for meeting the requirements. By simulation, different tools and strategies can be "tried out" in a fashion that will not compromise the current, on-going educational activity.

The Questions to Be Answered by an Educational System Analysis	The Steps in an Educational System Analysis
Where are we going and how do we know when we've arrived?	Determine mission objectives and performance requirements.
What are the things that will keep us from where we're going and how do we eliminate them?	Determine and reconcile constraints.
What are the major milestones along the way to where we're going?	Determine mission profile.
What are the "things" that must be done to get to each milestone?	Perform function analysis.
Of what specific tasks are the "things" composed?	Perform task analysis.
What are the possible ways of getting the "things" done?	Perform methods—means analysis.

FIG. 2.7. The questions to be answered in a system analysis and their relation to the steps of performing that analysis. After Kaufman (1968).

Step 4—implement solution strategy(ies): It is at the fourth system approach step that the products of planning and selection are actually accomplished. The methods and means are obtained, designed, adapted, or adopted. A management and control subsystem is developed to assure that everything will be available and utilized as required and that proper data will be collected to determine the extent to which the system is functioning as required. The system is put into operation, including all the complexities of utilization and acquisition of people, equipment, learners, facilities, budgets, and the many other factors necessary for a properly functioning educational system. Frequently network-based management techniques such as PERT (Program Evaluation Review Technique) and CPM (Critical Path Method) are quite useful in the management control of system implementation.

Step 5—determine performance effectiveness: Data are collected concerning both the process and the products of the system during and after the system's performance. Against the requirements established in the needs assessment and the detailed determination of requirements obtained from the system analysis, performance of the system is compared with the requirements. Discrepancies are noted between actual system performance and the performance requirements. This provides data on what is to be revised and thus gives diagnostic information that will permit valid system revision.

Step 6—revise system as required: Based on the performance of the system as indicated by the performance data, any or all previous system steps may be modified and a system redesign job accomplished if necessary. This self-correctional feature of a system approach assures constant relevance and practicality. An educational system is never considered to be complete, for it must be constantly evaluated in terms of:

1. Its ability to meet the needs and requirements it set out to respond to.
2. The continued appropriateness of its original needs and requirements. Thus we must have not only internal consistency and performance, but constant checking of needs and requirements to assure external validity as well.

Some Assumptions

A system approach as described here is nothing more than an application of logical problem solving that allows the educator to plan and manage relevant and practical educational outcomes. It requires that needs be formally identified and documented, and it starts the management process from a measurable referent. It then proceeds to identify requirements for meeting needs and identifies possible strategies and tools before the solution strategies and vehicles are actually selected. After the requirements and alternatives have been identified, the possible alternatives are selected, obtained, implemented, evaluated, and revised. A system approach is thus a self-correcting management process.

This paradigm of a system approach to education is a design process that is intended to be logical, orderly, systematic and self-correcting. It requires that the planner/analyst be open and objective and that only valid data be used in the planning, implementation, and evaluation. The following assumptions (Kaufman, 1970b) are included:

1. Needs can be identified and ultimately stated in measurable terms.
2. Human beings learn, and the type of learning opportunities and stimuli provided them can determine the directionality, at least, of this learning.
3. A systematic approach to educational problem solving will result in effectiveness and efficiency measurably greater than any other presently available process yields.
4. Attitudes and behaviors can be specified in measurable terms, at least by indicators of the classification of the behavior required.

5. It is better to try to state the existence of something and attempt to quantify it than it is to proclaim it as nonmeasurable and leave its existence and accomplishment still in question.

6. There is frequently a difference between hope and reality.

7. Teaching does not necessarily equal learning.

8. Educational areas that seem to defy quantification in system design offer prime areas for efforts in educational research.

9. A self-correcting system approach has greater utility than an open-loop process for achieving responsive education.

10. No system or procedure is ever the ultimate system. A system approach, like any other tool, should be constantly challenged and evaluated relative to other alternatives and should be revised or rejected when other tools prove more responsive and more useful.

If an educational manager desires to plan and design an education system "from scratch" without prejudging the adequacy of the current system, this model of a system approach can be a valuable tool—it does not automatically imply that the entire current system is wanting, and thus special precautions must be taken to assure that those portions of the educational system which are meeting the requirements are not discarded in the change process.

A system approach to education is a potentially useful tool for the educator who is willing to make the assumption that the overall job of an educational manager/administrator is to identify and solve educational problems in the most relevant and practical manner possible.

System Analysis Summary

System analysis, as we have noted, consists of a set of planning tools that tells *what* is to be done to meet identified and documented needs. Mission, function, and task analyses identify requirements for accomplishment; methods–means analysis identifies possible solution strategies and tools.

At the completion of system analysis, the planner has identified all of the feasible "whats" for problem solution, and he knows the possible ways and means for achieving each "what."

The usefulness of any system analysis lies in (1) the validity of the data it uses and (2) the objectivity and integrity of the planner.

System Analysis, System Approach, and Planning

A system approach, as described here, is a six-step process for realizing valid planned change. The six steps are quite general, and a self-correcting process is built into the approach. Thus the educator has a "road map" for achieving the desired change. The tools of system analysis may be used at each step of the process, and in fact are used to plan each step of a new educational program. The tools of needs assessment and system analysis may be used at each step of the process, and in fact are used to plan each step of a new educational program. The tools of needs assessment and system analysis are next presented in detail.

Glossary

Accountability: the ability to show that one has done what he said he would do.

Closed-loop process: a process that is self-correcting based on its performance or nonperformance. (In general system theory, this is frequently analogous to an "open system.")

Constraint: anything that will make it impossible to accomplish a performance requirement. Only if there are no possible methods and means for achieving a performance requirement is a constraint evident.

Educational management: a six-step process that includes the following elements:

1. Identify problem based on needs.

2. Determine solution requirements and solution alternatives.

3. Select solution strategy(ies) from among alternatives.

4. Implement selected strategies.

5. Determine performance effectiveness.

6. Revise as required, wherever required, whenever required.

Educational system planning: the identification of all requirements for meeting identified, documented needs. It includes the use of the tools associated with needs assessment and system analysis. When it is completed all the requirements and an identification of possible solution alternatives for designing, implementing, and achieving a responsive (and successful) educational system are present.

Function analysis: the analysis of each of the elements (functions) in the mission profile which shows what is to be done to complete each function. Function analysis is like a miniature mission analysis, that is specific to a smaller part of the overall problem. Like the mission analysis, it includes performance requirements (specifications) for the successful accomplishment of each function in the mission profile. Function analysis, however, depicts the subfunctions in the order and relationship necessary to successfully accomplish each function.

Management: a process for meeting needs.

Methods–means analysis: the determination of possible methods and means (strategies and tools) for accomplishing each performance requirement, and a listing of the relative advantages and disadvantages of each.

Mission analysis: the process for identifying, for the problem selected, the elements of (1) where are we going? (2) what criteria will we use to let us know when we have arrived? and (3) a management plan to show what functions must be performed to get us from where we are to where we are to be. This management plan is usually depicted in the form of a flow chart called a *mission profile.*

Open-loop process: a process that does not self-correct on the basis of performance. (In general system theory, this is frequently analogous to what is termed a "closed system.")

Performance requirement: a measurable specification for outcome. There may be two types of performance requirements—one that tells what the end product will look like or do, and another type that identifies specifications that are "given" relative to the manner in which the product is to be produced.

Problem: a documented discrepancy selected for resolution.

System analysis: a set of four related tools used for analyzing the requirements of a system that would, if satisfied, meet the identified need. The analysis identifies requirements (or specifications) for meeting the needs and the interrelations among the requirements; it also identifies potentially useful methods and means for meeting each requirement. The four related tools of system analysis are: mission analysis, function analysis, task analysis, and methods–means analysis. These tools are used to define the requirements (and thus define the problem) in increasing levels of detail and refinement.

Task analysis: the lowest level of system analysis. Task analysis shows, usually in tabular form (rather than flow chart form) the units of performance associated with each subfunction.

Exercises

1. What is accountability?
2. The tools of educational system analysis include:
   a. _____
   b. _____
   c. _____
   d. _____
3. In flow chart form, show the general (generic) problem-solving process model described in this book.
4. An educational system design procedure (a design process) must take the planner from _____ to _____ _____.
5. System analysis is primarily concerned with "_____ _____" whereas system synthesis is concerned with "_____ _____."

6. The sixth step of the problem-solving process, "revise as required," only happens after the fifth step, "determine performance effectiveness."

True _____

False _____

7. A system approach, as described here, is a process for _____
_____.

8. Why is a system approach suggested as a viable process for educational management?

determining educational needs

chapter 3

Both the requirement for needs assessment and the process characterizing it are receiving increased attention across the nation, with legislation for funding providing a good deal of the initial impetus. A partial list of state educational agencies which have or are now conducting assessments of educational needs include: Washington, Wisconsin, Pennsylvania, Utah, Michigan, Alabama, Montana, Tennessee, Minnesota, and Colorado.

In California alone, virtually every county and many cities (Temple City, San Francisco, San Jose, and Santa Barbara, to name a few) have conducted a formal delineation of needs. Sweigert (1969) has summarized many of the findings of the earlier California needs assessment activities.

Numerous approaches have been utilized to determine educational needs, ranging from asking teachers and educators what they think the needs are through development of questionnaires for educators, community leaders, and learners, and the obtaining of empirical learner performance data.

A Needs Assessment is a Discrepancy Analysis

The identification of needs is a discrepancy analysis that identifies the two polar positions of:

Where are we now?
Where are we to be?

and thus specifies the measurable discrepancy (or distance) between these two poles. It is critically important to the success of educational design that the data for marking these poles be as valid and representative as possible. The mere stating of goals does not endow them with validity. We can identify discrepancies endlessly and still fail to deal with the skills, knowledges, and attitudes that can serve learners in surviving and contributing when they leave school. A needs assessment (discrepancy analysis) must have at least three characteristics:

1. The data must represent the actual world of learners and related people, both as it exists now and as it will, could, and should exist in the future.

2. No needs determination is final and complete; we must realize that any statement of needs is in fact tentative, and we should constantly question the validity of our needs statements.

3. The discrepancies should be identified in terms of products or actual behaviors (ends), not in terms of processes (or means).

Avoiding the confusion of means and ends is central in needs assessment, for this error is a frequent cause of poor learning opportunities. Let us paraphrase Olguin's story concerning this important distinction, which is included in the 1970 White House Conference Report of the Forum on Educational Technology (which also recommended an analogous form of the six-step problem-solving model detailed in Chapter 2 and in this book):

Two men were walking down the street, and both spied simultaneously a rather large man. The two men turned to each other, and the first said, "Look at that fat man, he needs to go on a diet." The second man replied, "He is fat all right, but what he really needs is to jog!" The two men next went to talk to the subject of their discussion and said, "Hi, how do you feel?" The large man replied, "Well, not so good." The two men reveled for the moment in their excellent diagnosis and prescriptions. The large man continued, "I am the world champion weight lifter, and I have to put on about twenty or thirty more pounds so that I can press the amount of weight that it will take to win the next world competition. I won't feel really good until the extra weight is on me and I then know I can win the championship again!"

Our two hypothetical "needs assessors" would have been much better off to have ignored the process (diet, jog) and just assessed the discrepancy in terms of product! [Following the foregoing analogy, our would-be assessors could have noted that this man seemed to weigh in at 320 pounds and that the weight charts indicate that even a large-boned man of his height should have weighed about 190 pounds. Then they could have checked for the discrepancy in this *individual case* based on the unique characteristics and requirements of the individual involved.] It is critical, therefore, that we not only identify needs as discrepancies in terms of products (or outcomes) but that we never leap to the solution or infer it as part of a needs assessment (or discrepancy analysis). There are differences between "need," "want," "desire," and "require." When we use the word "need" as a verb we are usually risking our jumping to a solution before defining the problem. Einstein once stated, "perfection of means and confusion of goals seem—in my opinion—to characterize our age."

So far as possible, in conducting a discrepancy analysis (needs assessment), we should include all the educational partners in attempting to achieve educational success. These partners include, at least:

1. The learners.
2. The parents and community members.
3. The educators (or implementers of the educational process).

An effort to determine needs that does not include all the partners in education runs the risk of presenting a seriously biased starting point for educational design. Data from, and participation of, these partners may be obtained in many ways, including the setting up of panels and the use of various methods of interview and questionnaires. Current needs assessment procedures vary. Some start from a determination of "felt" needs, whereas others intend to identify needs based on "hard" empirical data of discrepancies. It is suggested that needs based on "hard" empirical data (i.e., data collected from the operational world) will have greater utility for educational system design than "opinion" data or listings of "felt needs."

Three Possible Dimensions for a Needs Assessment

One proposed model for assessing educational needs (Kaufman, Corrigan, and Johnson 1969) is partially based on a formulation by Hanna (1966) concerning three equally important foci of curriculum; nature of knowledge, nature of learner, and nature of society. This model suggests that the logical entry point, if there is to be one, is through the dimension of "nature of society." However, each dimension should be considered, and discrepancies for each variable should be collected and documented. This needs assessment model emphasizes the interactive nature of several sources of needs in a responsive educational system.

A further refinement of this model may be considered (see Fig. 3.1). In this restatement, the "gatekeeper" of educational change is formally considered, and thus the needs assessment dimension of the "nature of

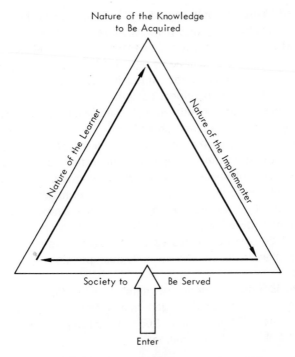

Nature of the Knowledge
to Be Acquired

Nature of the Learner

Nature of the Implementer

Society to   Be Served

Enter

**FIG. 3.1.   A diagrammatic representation of the relation among
three critical variables for educational assessment of needs
[suggested modification of model presented by Kaufman, Corrigan, and Johnson (1969)]. The internal arrows indicate that at
least these three dimensions must be considered in concert in
any viable assessment of needs. This figure also identifies the
suggested interrelationship, cooperation, and active participation of at least three groups of educational partners: learners,
implementers, and society.**

the educator" is included.[1] According to this reformulation, the "nature
of knowledge" is considered only after the needs from the dimensions
of society, the learner, and the educator have been determined.

Using such a needs assessment model, the educational planner would
identify and document discrepancies in each of the three dimensions,
thereafter attempting to reconcile any discrepancies among the three
variables. For instance, a discrepancy between "what is" and "what should
be" for the variables of the society to be served and the implementing
educator might be that furnished by the Harris Poll (*Life magazine*, 1969):

*1.   This model could be adapted to the preschool learner by changing this
dimension to "nature of the implementer" and thus including parents when they
work with their own children at home.*

when asked "What schools should do?" 62 percent of the parents polled stated that "maintaining discipline is more important than student self-inquiry," whereas 27 percent of the teachers cited that item. Thus a discrepancy exists between a need as perceived by "the society to be served" and the "nature of the educator." It is this type of discrepancy which must be reconciled before educational design may reasonably proceed.

When determining needs in the dimension of "the society to be served," the decision reached should not represent the "freezing" of the status quo for its own sake, followed by the issuance of requirements to make our learners "fit in." Rather, it is important to capture the current and future status of society, thus providing learners with the skills, abilities, and attitudes to make a better place for all mankind.

A fundamental assumption of educational system planning is that it is a human and humane process that starts in a context of values and valuing and derives its successes and failures in terms of the extent to which any plan is responsive to individual people with unique patterns of values.

In considering the three "partners" in educational planning and accomplishment, it is strongly urged that a formal determination of each group's values be undertaken. Such a starting values analysis might include the following determination:

1. Determine the current values of each of the partners.
2. Determine the desired values of each partner as he himself perceives them.
3. Determine the perceptions of each partner concerning the values of the other partners, both currently and in the future.
4. Determine the matches and mismatches between these differential current and future perceptions of values to form a central part of the initial discrepancy analysis.

Match/Mismatch Analysis

This type of analysis is simply a determination of the compatibilities and incompatibilities that exist in obtained data. If the partners have basic disagreements in values, goals, and/or objectives, this will be spotlighted by an analysis of matches and mismatches in obtained representative data. If there are "matches," it is probably safe to proceed; mismatches indicate that better mutual understanding should be obtained, which ought to result in greater congruity between values, goals, and objectives.

Types of Needs Assessment Models

At least three types of needs assessment procedures or models may be identified (Kaufman and Harsh, 1969); an inductive model (type I), a deductive model (type D) and a "classical" model (type C). They differ primarily in terms of their starting point for the determination of the goals and objectives for education. Fig. 3.2, taken from Kaufman and Harsh's article, represents the three types of procedural models.

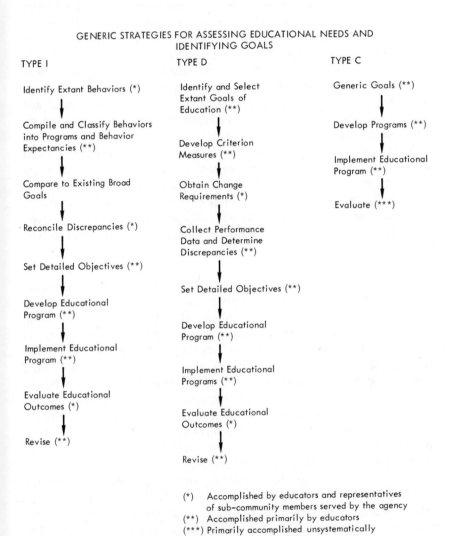

GENERIC STRATEGIES FOR ASSESSING EDUCATIONAL NEEDS AND IDENTIFYING GOALS

TYPE I

Identify Extant Behaviors (*)
↓
Compile and Classify Behaviors into Programs and Behavior Expectancies (**)
↓
Compare to Existing Broad Goals
↓
Reconcile Discrepancies (*)
↓
Set Detailed Objectives (**)
↓
Develop Educational Program (**)
↓
Implement Educational Program (**)
↓
Evaluate Educational Outcomes (*)
↓
Revise (**)

TYPE D

Identify and Select Extant Goals of Education (**)
↓
Develop Criterion Measures (**)
↓
Obtain Change Requirements (*)
↓
Collect Performance Data and Determine Discrepancies (**)
↓
Set Detailed Objectives (**)
↓
Develop Educational Program (**)
↓
Implement Educational Programs (**)
↓
Evaluate Educational Outcomes (*)
↓
Revise (**)

TYPE C

Generic Goals (**)
↓
Develop Programs (**)
↓
Implement Educational Program (**)
↓
Evaluate (***)

(*)   Accomplished by educators and representatives of sub-community members served by the agency
(**) Accomplished primarily by educators
(***) Primarily accomplished unsystematically

FIG. 3.2. Three different models for determining educational needs. Type I is basically inductive, type D is basically deductive, and type C is intended to be representative of "classical" educational procedures for identifying and defining goals and objectives. After Kaufman and Harsh (1969).

Inductive model (type I):   The inductive model derives its name from the fact that the goals, expectancies, and outcomes for education are first obtained from the members of the subcommunities in the district, and the program is based on these data. The first job in using this model is to see how the learners in the district are behaving now. In the district that pioneered this approach (Newport–Mesa Unified School District in California; Shuck, 1968) Flanagan's critical incident technique (1954) was employed to determine from various representative community strata behaviors that indicated (1) that the schools were doing an unsatisfactory job and (2) that the schools were doing a satisfactory job. Next, these critical incidents were compiled and sorted into program areas and behavior expectancies that would represent the behaviors identified by the various subcommunities in the district.

The next chores would be to compare these expectancies with existing broad goals of education (district goals, etc.), to reconcile any discrepancies in a manner acceptable to the various subcommunities, and then to set detailed objectives for bringing about the required behaviors. From these detailed objectives, the educational program would be developed, implemented, evaluated against the detailed objectives, and revised as necessary.

Deductive model (type D):   The deductive model starts from existing goals and outcome statements and proceeds to "deduce" an educational program from this initial material. When using this model, the starting point is the identification and selection of existing goals of education. In the innovating school district (Temple City Unified School District in California; Kaufman, Rand, English, Conte, and Hawkins, 1968) educators surveyed available goal formulations and selected the one done by the Pennsylvania State Department of Instruction and Educational Testing Service (1965). From these ten proposed goals of education, criterion measures (actually indicators) were developed that would be representative of certain behaviors; when these behaviors were observed, the successful accomplishment of the different goals would be indicated.

The next step would be to obtain change requirements from the various partners in the educational system (in Temple City the partners were learners, educators, and community members; in Newport–Mesa these were categorized somewhat differently as "subcommunities"). Then actual performance data would be collected concerning the extent to which the criteria (indicators) were or were not being realized. Based on the obtained discrepancies, detailed objectives are next set, and an appropriate educational program is developed, implemented, evaluated, and revised.

"Classical" model (type C):   This model is the one most often used, usually by default, by educational agencies today. It is not recommended. It usually starts with some general statements of goals or intents and proceeds directly to the development of educational programs, which are implemented and evaluated. Usually none of the four major elements in this effort is accomplished on the basis of empirical data, nor is work performed precisely and measurably.

There is no clear choice to be made between the type I model and the type D model. Each has distinct advantages and disadvantages, and thus—as with most other decisions to be made concerning needs assessment—a selection should be made on the basis of the unique characteristics of the educational agency and the community it serves.

The type I model is valuable because it starts with the perceptions and concerns of the partners in the immediate school area, but it has the disadvantage of being somewhat slower and more complex to implement than the type D process. A number of different tools for implementing each of the functions identified with both the type D and the type I models may be considered for use, and some of these are presented in this chapter.

An Example of Goal Indicators

The "Ten Proposed Goals for Education" (1965) developed by Educational Testing Service (ETS) and the Pennsylvania State Department of Instruction suggests a useful starting referent for devising a deductive model. Although these goals are not now formulated in operational terms, they do represent the distillation of perceptions of a statewide sample. The needs assessment efforts of the Temple City Unified School District (1968) used the "Ten Proposed Goals" and developed measurable "indicators" for each goal. These index measures serve as a reaction baseline for the educational partners.

The following indicators for the fourth Pennsylvania/ETS goal— "Quality education should help every child acquire a positive attitude toward school and toward the learning process"—furnish an example of the preliminary index measures identified in the Temple City effort:

A. At each grade level learners will individually and collectively display behavior which will:

   1. Reduce unexcused absences by 10 percent as compared with previous year's attendance records.

   2. Reduce unexcused tardiness by 10 percent as compared with previous year's attendance and punctuality records.

3. Increase number of books and numbers and kinds of media used in libraries and instructional materials centers checked out and used by learners by 10 percent each year as compared with the previous year.

4. Reduce recorded discipline problems (students sent to office, kept after school, etc.) by 10 percent each year as compared with the previous year.

5. Reduce by at least 10 percent per year the number of defacings of school properties and materials as compared with the previous year's records. This will include such indicators as number of textbooks defaced, broken windows, and graffiti.

6. Improve by at least 5 percent per year the average score on an attitude questionnaire given to learners which is designed to assess learner attitudes toward (a) school and (b) learning.

B. After graduation, when asked, previous learners will:

1. Indicate at least 10 percent above previous year that what they had learned was important and useful.

2. Indicate at least 10 percent above previous year that learning experiences at TCUSD (Temple City Unified School District) were enjoyable.

3. Continue education [adult education courses, college and university attendance (either part or full time), specialty courses and occupational courses] at a rate which increases at least 5 percent above the previous year.

4. Number of books used and borrowed in TCUSD public libraries will increase at least 5 percent each year after the initiation of this program (to indicate improved attitude toward school and learning) as compared with the previous year.

5. Obtain increasing support budget and program expansion for improved education.

These crude indicators are not intended to be complete, collectively or individually. Rather, they are intended to be gross indicators of the domain to which they are related with the requirement that further refinement, testing, and evaluation will provide hard data relative to their utility and revision. However, these indicators do supply a possible starting point for a performance-based decision procedure.

A Utility Referent for Needs Assessment

A possible starting referent for needs assessment has been offered by Kaufman, Corrigan, and Johnson (1969). They suggest a utility model with an overall goal for education that, by the time the learner has finished he should be able to survive and, ideally, to contribute. To measure this "survival" they suggest that an indicator could be an economic one, where survival is defined as the point at which an individual's consumption equals his production. For the purposes of their utility model, they propose that "consumption," in our society at least, be measured by money spent and that "production" be measured by money received.

Kaufman and co-workers present a utility continuum with a variable midpoint (fixed by society and subject to change by the dictates of society), a zone called "dependent survival," and a zone called "contribution" (see Fig. 3.3). Any individual at any time is at some point on this continuum—at the independent survival point (where production is equal to consumption), in the dependent survival zone (where production is less than consumption), or in the contribution zone (where production is greater than consumption). Using this model, an educator interested in designing an educational system to achieve at least minimal outcomes for its learners could plot where an individual currently is and where he should be. Thus measurable discrepancies between actual and desired results could be derived.

Not readily apparent in the model, but included by virtue of reality and inference, is the inclusion of many humanistic requirements in surviving and contributing. The formulations of many humanists, including Maslow (1968), Frankl (1962, 1965, 1967, 1969), Rogers (1964), and Rucker (1969), may be expressed in this model. Under this formulation, the greater

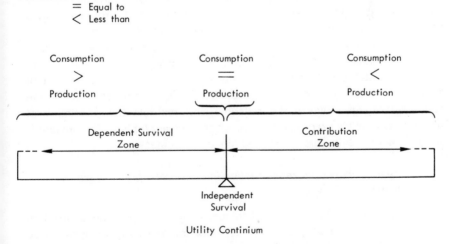

FIG 3.3. A proposed continuum of individual utility in our society. After Kaufman, Corrigan, and Johnson (1969).

an individual's ability to realize his own uniqueness, the greater the possibility for him to be at or beyond the "independent survival" point. Fully functioning, self-actualizing people, will, it is suggested, contribute more, as measured by the criteria in this model.

A Needs Assessment Is Never Completed

Any needs assessment procedure must be a continuing affair. The operational world to which educational agencies attempt to be responsive is dynamic, and changes in needs are to be expected. A needs assessment should not become "cast in concrete" but should receive constant attention to assure that relevant needs are identified and included in the educational system design and revision process.

Selecting the Needs—Defining the Problem

After needs have been determined (and stated in discrepancy terms), they may be ordered and selected. Frequently, a community panel or other sampling of representative groups may be utilized to place priorities among the identified and documented needs. This priority setting is important because there never seems to be enough money and time (and other resources) for meeting all the identified needs in any educational agency's realm of activity. Resources and funds must be allocated to the projects with the highest priority and the highest payoff. Some priority-setting criteria must be invoked, such as rating each need in terms of "cost of meeting the need" and "cost of ignoring the need." Based on the priorities assigned to the array of identified needs, those with the highest priority are tagged for action. The needs identified and selected by an educational agency become the system problems. A problem is thus defined as: a documented discrepancy selected for resolution.

It has been said that a needs assessment is a discrepancy analysis— the documentation of a measurable difference between current and desired or required states of affairs. Preconceived solutions must be left out of such declarations of discrepancies, for the inclusion of a "solution" in the statement of need biases the outcome and restricts the possibility of utilizing innovative or creative ways of solving a problem. For instance, what is *wrong* with this attempted needs statement:

We need to individualize instruction in the second grade class at Plakos Elementary School.

Well, we can criticize several things. First, although individualization of instruction is probably an important *tool* for achieving many required educational results, it still is a *solution*; and we have not yet identified the discrepancies between "what is" and "what should be" for the learners involved, nor have we bothered to determine what all the partners (what happened to the input of the learner and the community member?) in education have said that they value. Other weaknesses in this needs statement include the lack of a measurable discrepancy in terms of learner behaviors, and the failure to supply a criterion for when this should be accomplished.

Let us examine another hypothetical attempt to formulate a needs statement:

Measurably improve learner performance in reading by using validated self-instructional materials in phonics and linguistic structures in the third grade of the F. W. English Elementary School.

This example is a bit better in that quantification is noted in the statement. However, there is no documentation of a discrepancy; the source of the implied goal of reading, is not identified; and solution elements (phonics and linguistics) are included, before the discrepancy has been noted and alternative possible solutions have been identified and considered. Also, there should have been some criterion for when the program is to be completed.

What about:

The community members, educators, and learners in the Mayrhofer Unified School District have decided that reading skills and abilities are the critical priority item in the district, and that the current elementary learners have a mean score of 42nd percentile on the valid Fikes Test of Reading Ability and demonstrate a standard deviation of 15. Because of this it has been mandated by the school board that by one year from this date that the mean reading score on the same test will be at or above the 55th percentile with a standard deviation not to exceed 10.

If we do not question the advisability of using standardized test instruments, then this is a usable needs statement featuring a measurable discrepancy between where one is and where one should be that is based on performance data. Note that such a needs statement identifies the elements of "what is" and "what should be" in measurable performance terms; thus it includes the elements usually suggested in descriptions of behavioral (or performance) objectives. A needs statement is like any other performance objective in that it states for terminal conditions: (1) what is to be achieved, (2) by whom the outcome is to be displayed, (3) under what conditions, and (4) what criteria will be used to measure success. Moreover, it states these dimensions *both* for "what is" (the starting conditions) *and* for "what should be" (the finishing conditions).

Formulating and Documenting Needs

Sometimes it is helpful to list documentation and data for the two elements of a needs statement:

What is:
A needs assessment has documented a discrepancy in reading ability as measured by the Fikes test. Validation data have shown that the Fikes test is appropriate.
Current elementary school learner performance on this test shows a mean performance at the 42nd percentile with a standard deviation of 15.
School board resolution of September 24 has mandated a measurable improvement within a "short time."

What should be:
By one year from this date learners in the Mayrhofer elementary school should have shown measurable improvement.
Measurable improvement will be taken as no less than a mean score of 55th percentile with a standard deviation not to exceed 10.
The same test instrument will be used.

In identifying needs, documentation in the form of empirical data is encouraged. For instance, if you have chosen a standardized test, it would be useful to have some validation data for that test to support the use of that particular test with that learner (target) population. These data would help the reviewer or independent educational accomplishment auditor determine the viability of the need and ascertain if the criteria measures used were really appropriate. Unfortunately, but realistically, sometimes opinion information from "experts" are the only data available; if this is the case, such data may be used to tentatively substantiate elements in a needs statement.

Noting that any needs assessment should formally consider the interacting variables of discrepancies for learners, society, and implementers, we could suggest a format for listing discrepancies that would include the formal listing of discrepancies in each of these three domains. One such listing might summarize the information from a needs assessment in table form. The data recorded in Table 3.1 (as well as all other examples in this book) are hypothetical.

As we note later in our discussion of mission analysis (Chapter 4), there is an integral relation between the statement of a need and the mission objective. The same techniques are used, and the requirements for measurability are the same. The difference is that a needs statement documents the measurable discrepancy between "what is" and "what should be," whereas the mission objective only states "what should be."

TABLE 3.1   Possible Needs Assessment Summary Table (Hypothetical)

What Is (Current Condition)	What Should Be (Required Condition)
1. Learner: The drop-out rate among Mexican–American learners in this school district is currently X percent. The current drop-out rate among all other groups is U percent. etc.	1. Learner: The drop-out rate for Mexican-Americans should not be greater than that of any other groups. etc.
2. Implementer: R percent of credentialed teachers have no capability to speak Spanish, and T percent of the learners entering are unable to speak any English. etc.	2. Implementer: All Spanish-speaking learners should have continual access to a Spanish-speaking credentialed teacher, and thus at least B percent of all teachers and C percent of all staff should be able to speak Spanish to the S level. etc.
3. Society: English is required in this community in order to seek and obtain employment at the subsistence level or better as defined by the Department of Labor report XX-5-77. etc.	3. Society: All learners legally exiting from this district should be able, if desired, to seek and obtain employment for at least one year's duration, which will be at or above the subsistence level as defined by the same Department of Labor report or that in the same series which might replace it within the next five years. etc.

Some Other Useful Models

Assessing needs is not new; many have participated in the exercise of stating where one should be going based on where he is now. Let us now discuss some additional models that may be considered by an educator interested in conducting an assessment of educational needs.

The Sweigert model: In a detailed statement entitled "The First Step in Educational Problem Solving—A Systematic Assessment of Student Benefits," Sweigert (1969) provides a process for determining a possible starting point for educational design. He suggests the following characteristics for a statement of needs: (1) focus on student needs, (2) identification of target groups of students, (3) criteria for evaluating progress toward meeting the need, (4) criticality of need, (5) size of statement (level of generality), and (6) current commitment of funds. Sweigert suggests a matrix which includes the following "partners":

1. Any given student.

2. Any appropriate representative of the public school agency operating the school attended by the student.

3. The consumer of the educational product.

He then compares responses of these three groups on the perceived importance of specific learning objectives and plots the matches and mismatches among the various groups to determine the likelihood of successful attainment based on the patterns of acceptance and rejection. He offers an analysis of various types of patterns of acceptances and rejections of commonly considered objectives (also see Sweigert, 1971).

It is suggested that this type of model can be a powerful tool in identifying areas of concern. This type of "concerns analysis" may be extremely useful in placing in perspective the vast array of possible goals and the importance attached to each goal by each partner in the educational process. One potentially helpful extension of this methodology might be the collection of empirical data after this "concerns analysis" has been completed, in order to determine the extent to which the concerns are "real" in terms of the existence of discrepancies between current performance and required performance.

The Rucker model: Referring to the contributions of Maslow (1968), Axtelle (1966), Rogers (1964), and Laswell (1948), Rucker (1969) presents "a value-oriented framework" for education and the behavioral sciences. According to his model, there are eight value categories representing a range of valuing events from the deepest personal to the most complex societal concerns. They include love, respect, skill, understanding, influence, goods and services, well-being, and responsibility. These value categories as defined by Rucker could assist us in naming and defining the areas of concern and of required accomplishment for an educational needs assessment.

Of additional utility is a possible determination of current self-concept and desired self-concept and/or purpose in life (cf. Crumbaugh & Maholick, 1969, which discusses possible assessment procedures based, in part, on Frankl's concept of "existential vacuum").

The CIPP model: Although he is primarily concerned with evaluation, Stufflebeam (1968) has suggested a model that is worth consideration by educators (also see Randall, 1969). This paradigm, termed the CIPP (Context, Input, Process, Product) evaluation model, includes the elements of:

1. Context evaluation—the systematic analysis of the demographic, cultural, historical, and socio-economic factors related to the problem. Also included here is an environmental analysis, a description of the area in which the changes are to occur.

2. Input evaluation—studies of facilities, personnel, services, and the like which are available for use in any program.

3. Process evaluation—procedures employed, including se-quences, conditions, and roles of components in the program.

4. Product evaluation—the extent to which objectives were at-tained, including unintended changes or results.

As Harsh points out in his contribution to "A Plan for Planning for the Inglewood Unified School District [Chenney, Harsh, Kaufman, Shuck, and Wood, (1970)], planning and evaluation are inextricably related. The CIPP model emphasizes the requirement to determine the context and inputs to a program before beginning; it also stresses the necessity of including these elements in any evaluation of the utility of the program used.

Using the Needs Assessment Information

Regardless of the discrepancy analysis model or tools utilized, there comes a time when there may be more data than one knows what to do with. Data for their own sake have marginal usefulness, so the design of the data collection process should include consideration of what data are desired, what one wants to do with them, and how the data are to be handled to provide the necessary information for educational design.

After discrepancies have been identified and documented, we must decide which discrepancies are of sufficient priority to merit inclusion in the educational system design. Generally this requires choosing from among the array of discrepancies (needs), since there are never enough resources and time to deal with all identified and documented needs.

Several options are available, and the reader may well design his own based on the characteristics of his educational system and its par-ticipants. One possibility is to use the concerns analysis of Sweigert (1969) described earlier in this chapter.

Another possibility is to identify a stratified sample of the "partners" in educational success in the given educational agency's area and have them select the priorities for the array of documented needs. Such a sorting might be made by the individuals on the basis of two criteria, both generally judgmental:

1. What does it cost to meet the need?

2. What does it cost to ignore the need?

Individual sortings of needs can then be compared to determine consensus, and any gross differences can be negotiated among the part-ners. Complete consensus is almost never attained (and perhaps it should not be attained), and the educational manager himself should decide how much agreement is necessary to proceed. (One might hazard that consensus among at least 51 percent of each of the partner groups—parents and community, learners, and educators—would be necessary to begin).

Some Steps in Conducting a Needs Assessment

The following tools and procedures for conducting a needs assessment might vary depending on who is doing the planning, where the planning is being accomplished, and other requirements concerning each educational agency and context.

1. Decide to plan.

2. Identify problem symptoms or obtain a request for a needs assessment from the educational agency.

3. Identify the domain for planning (e.g. a school district, a school, a class, an individual learner).

4. Identify possible needs assessment tools and procedures, select the best one(s), and obtain the participation of the partners in planning including learners, community members and parents, and implementers (usually educators).

5. Determine the existing condition, with prime focus on the learner, his physical, mental, and developmental characteristics, and including the elements of the context in which change is to occur, including the society and the implementer(s). Make sure that the existing conditions are stated in measurable performance terms.

6. Determine required condition, again with prime focus on the learner. These, too, should be in measurable performance terms.

7. Reconcile any discrepancies that exist between the planning partners, identifying the needs so that there is consensus of learners, society, and implementers.

8. Place priorities among the discrepancies and select those on which action will be taken.

9. Make sure that the needs assessment process is a continuing procedure to assure that the educational design job will always be up to date, consistently reflecting the real world of the learners and their educational partners.

Getting the data: The tools for obtaining data for the needs assessment are as many and varied as the number of educational agencies. The tools selected must yield information that truly represents the two polar conditions of "what is" and "what should be." For instance, when educational partners are asked to list their goals for education, they frequently name solutions and not goals (e.g., "we should have more individualized instruction in our schools . . .''). Therefore, instruments should be designed to elicit *outcome* information. Most existing statements of goals for educational agencies are either in terms of process or are so general that they cannot meaningfully form the starting point for educational design.

Another tendency is for participants to conform to the group norm. One method that seems to hold increasing utility for such goal setting and prediction of future events has been termed the Delphi technique (cf. Dalkey, 1970). Basically, the Delphi technique eliminates group and open debate activities, substituting a precise and carefully designed series of questions supported with information. A representative group (e.g., a stratified sample of representative community members, learners, and educators in a school district) is selected and solicited for their participation, and a commitment for cooperation is obtained. The Delphi process as described by Dalkey involves four general ideas: anonymity, iteration, controlled feedback, and statistical group response.

In the implementation of the Delphi technique, according to this formulation, there is a collection of responses to questionnaire items. From this set of responses, information is fed back to the group in a controlled fashion, usually a number of times. Finally, there is a "completed" product, which is a statistical group response weighing the responses of all individuals but with an indication of normative outcomes. Thus the Delphi technique yields a group response to prestated questions or items that are considered important or relevant to a given question, such as might be desired in a needs assessment.

This tool for group inquiry and prediction avoids some of the biases normally introduced in other group methods of obtaining information from the various partners in education concerning future conditions of society and for education. Other less complex instruments are available anywhere from the construction of a questionnaire or interview format to the publishing of requests for information in local newspapers.

Educational planning starts with needs assessment, and therefore the planner should begin by finding out which instruments may be used for determining what the situation is and what it should be.

One method of proceeding is to identify what the expected outcomes should be (through questionnaires, panels, or the like) and to state them in measurable terms, such as the goal indicators shown earlier for Temple City (p. 35). Then, against each of these indicators, an investigation is completed which measurably indicates the current situation, usually in terms of learner skills, knowledges, and attitudes, as well as behaviors of the other partners, the educators, and the community. From this basic tabulation, the discrepancies may be listed, documented, and compared.

It would be inappropriate to list a "hard and fast" process along with tools for doing a needs assessment, for the procedures are too new and are constantly evolving. Tools and techniques for needs assessment must be selected, evolved, or invented based on the unique conditions and circumstance of each educational context.

The field of needs assessment is indeed a fledgling one. Many models and procedures are being tried, modified, and reapplied. Professionals specializing in this difficult area emphasize the tentative nature of any models or procedures extant. This presentation is no exception, for we simply do not know very much about this very important subject. However, rather than skipping it because there are no cast-in-concrete how-to-do-it prescriptions, a better choice would be to design one (perhaps using the system analysis tools described in this book) to fit individual educational requirements. Following is a set of tools that might be considered in conducting an educational assessment of needs.

Some Suggested Tools and Procedures for Conducting a
Needs Assessment

1. Decide to plan: Group decision to plan made by all the partners in education, (implementers, learners, and community). Tools could include group presentation and vote, or could utilize an explanation in writing, along with a ballot, followed by a publication of the results of balloting. Other possibilities include convening representative panels based on a sample of the constituency of the partners and asking for their recommendations and approval.

2. Identify problem symptoms or obtain a request for a needs assessment from the educational agency: Since this could be either a precursor or a follow-up on the decision to plan, step 2 is interchangeable with step 1. If a request is given for a needs assessment, then step 2 may be skipped; otherwise the problem symptoms harvested might provide the information necessary to obtain the charter to begin to plan by using a needs assessment. Tools could include a simple reporting of incidents that have occurred recently in the educational context—for example, a listing of such things as incidence of drug use, defacings, drop-outs, and the like. One could use statistics of the school agency and reports by teachers, parents, or others.

3. Identify the domain for planning: Here the decision is to be made (and it can always be expanded or contracted—planning and a system approach are revisable activities) concerning whether the planning should be for an individual child, a class, a school, a district, a county, a state, and so on. Again, any tool utilized should include all the educational partners, by either direct or representative participation and vote.

4. Identify possible needs assessment tools and procedures and select the best ones: This is a tricky area, since there are no hard-and-fast procedures. It might be desirable to ask an expert in this growing field or perhaps to read the literature, assessing the characteristics of your arena and selecting the most appropriate possibilities; or one might want to do both. The ever-increasing literature in this area should be reviewed extensively.

Here the outcomes of needs assessment are stated in measurable performance terms, including all the criteria used in any measurable objective. Criteria usually associated with programmed instruction and learning objectives are useful here. The assessment objectives should include outcomes for at least the three partners of education, and they should list objectives within each of these categories.

Because one is dealing with the overlapping concerns of many individuals when a needs assessment is performed, be sure that all the partners are involved in the selection and decision. Many people, perhaps unjustifiably, feel that the only "partner" that should be assessed in detail is the learner—we are used to doing that. Another partner might feel that by allowing himself to be assessed, he permits the assessors to invade his privacy—needs assessment tends to be perceived as something that is a good idea for someone else. Never select instruments that affix blame or could be used to do so—a needs assessment is a process for helping all the partners in education, not to harm or hinder anyone or any group.

5. Determine the existing condition for all the partners: A number of tools are useful here; again it might be desirable to select from among these, modify some, or design one's own.

For determining the values of the partners, Rucker's values analysis procedure (1969) holds promise. Also, Sweigert's model for determining starting concerns (1968) is useful here (as well as in the next step). The CIPP model also can help to define some crucial parameters. Another useful method for determining the perceptions of existing conditions is through the use of Flannagan's (1954) critical incident technique. Yet another referent could be the utility criteria suggested by Kaufman, Corrigan, and Johnson (1969).

Also of use are the myriads of publications concerning the current status of learners, community members, and educators—the 1970 White House Conference on Children published a useful compendium concerning children, and other sources might include census data, reports from city planning agencies, and other extant actuarial data.

6. Determine required condition: This is perhaps the most difficult in planning and needs assessment, for it is tempting either to install one's own biases or to depend on an incomplete or unbalanced set of outcome expectancies. Again, it is of vital importance to include all the educational partners in this determination and to involve them in the decision process, not at some later time, when they are forced to react, not having had a positive active role in the beginning.

Sweigert's model can be employed once more in determining the degree of consensus on sample goals and objectives. Also, Rucker's values analysis which identifies eight-value categories may supply perceived points in valuing behavior that each individual desires for himself and/or for others. The Kaufman, Corrigan, and Johnson utility criterion could be useful for stating one of the outcome requirements. Additionally, there exist numerous statements of goals for education—from that of your local district to the simple and homely "Seven Cardinal Principles of Education" (familiar to virtually everyone who has endured a single education course), to elaborate determinations such as those accomplished by the Pennsylvania State Department of Instruction and the Educational Testing Service. (Frequently, statements of goals and objectives are not in measurable or behavioral terms. When this is the case, the "partners" might desire to derive indicators—behaviors typical and representative of that type or class of behaviors intended by the goal—for each of the broadly stated goals; thus it would be possible to set some measurable specifications for expected or desired goals and outcomes of education.)

Part of step 6 includes the requirement to state outcomes for the future, since we should not attempt to capture the status quo and derive an education system to maintain that status. This is a bit like crystal ball gazing, but "gaze we must," to prepare our children for a better tomorrow. To help predict the future, there are a number of increasingly better writings on this topic, including Harman's "Nature of Our Changing Society: Implications for Schools" (1970). Review and make an analysis of as many of these written predictions as possible. Another tool for forecasting includes the Delphi technique, the previously noted method of individualized determination for a group prediction.

7. Reconcile any discrepancies among the partners' viewpoints: This is easier said than done, but well worth the investment in time and effort. Of possible use here would be the procedure of convening representative panels or groups and asking them to reconcile any discrepancies that exist among the partners. (Sweigert's model, especially, will reveal any mismatches quite graphically.)

A less courageous method would be to select only those outcomes in which there already exists a consensus that is deemed high enough to warrant proceeding. Of some comfort for those considering this alternative is the perception that differences between groups that seem to be violently opposed often are reduced when needs are discussed in terms of outcomes rather than in terms of procedures or processes.

8. Place priorities among the discrepancies and select: Again, representative panels or even a large group ballot might be used to set priorities among the identified and reconciled discrepancies. Of considerable usefulness here is to request that priorities be placed based on two simultaneous questions—"what does it cost to meet this need" and "what does it cost to ignore this need?"

9. Make sure the needs assessment is a continuing process: The best tool here is a leadership which insists on this step as a requirement for providing relevant education. An agency within the school organization can be set up to perform this continuous function, or it might be stated in policy that the needs assessment will be updated and corrected periodically. Perhaps most useful would be a planning and evaluation agency within the school organization which has as one of its key functions and responsibilities the performance of a continuous needs assessment.

Needs Assessment Summary

An educational *need* is a measurable outcome discrepancy between "what is" and "what should be." If there is no difference between where we are and where we should be, then we have no "need."

Measurable is a key word, for it is not enough to guess or intuit either where we are or where we should be—we require hard empirical data for both polar positions of a need.

Needs assessment is a process for obtaining such discrepancy data and for placing priorities among them. The data for needs assessment are best when information is obtained from the "real world," which exists outside of education. Intuition and hunches have little utility in a needs assessment.

At least three types of needs assessment models have been identified:

1. Deductive models (type D).
2. Inductive models (type I).
3. Classical models.

The deductive model starts with a predetermined list of objectives or outcomes (usually only indicators because full and complete lists of objectives are not within the current state of the art). These objectives are derived from values and empirical data concerning "what is" and "what should be." Partners in the educational process—community members, educators (implementers), and learners—utilize these lists in order to determine their utility, their completeness, and their accuracy. From these lists are derived the goals for education, and data are collected to determine the extent to which there are actual discrepancies.

The inductive model starts with the partners in education, and they, individually and/or in groups, determine the values and resulting goals for education. The partners make lists and place priorities among them, and then collect data on how well or how poorly these goals are being accomplished.

A classical model of identifying needs is not recommended.

After needs are identified, using either the type D or type I process, one does no more than select from among all the discrepancies those requiring action. Thus a priority setting procedure is necessary to select those needs of the highest priority.

Priority selection may be made by panels of concerned partners in education. Useful criteria for sorting needs into action priorities include the cost of meeting the need and the cost of ignoring the need.

After priorities have been placed among the needs, they are usually listed in descending order of importance and then each in turn is slated for action, based on the budget available.

Selecting relevant variables for the needs assessment is critical. It has been suggested that three variables, at least, should be considered:

1. The nature of the society.
2. The nature of the learner.
3. The nature of the implementer (or educator).

Normally, at least the discrepancy data corresponding to the current situation and the required situation are determined for each of the three dimensions. All discrepancies should then be reconciled. [Other schemes are available for dimensionalizing these variables, e.g., Stufflebeam's CIPP (Context, Input, Product, Process) variables model (1968) and Sweigert's model.]

Glossary

Delphi technique: a method useful for forecasting which obtains judgmental data concerning future events using anonymous panels which obtain information concerning the responses of others to previous questions.

Discrepancy analysis: another term for needs assessment; the process of determining and documenting a measurable difference between two states of affairs, one of which is hypothesized. In the case of a needs assessment, the analysis documents measurable differences between the polar positions of "what is" and "what should be," or what are the current outcomes and what are the required outcomes.

Indicator: a behavior or class of behaviors that signal that a larger goal or objective is being met. Use of indicators in needs assessment is a tacit statement that we cannot measure all behaviors that are representative of a goal or objective and that we will use representative behaviors (or indicators) to determine if the goal or objective is being met.

Type C model: a needs assessment model that is "classical" or customary in most educational agencies. It starts with generic goals, usually set by educators alone.

Type D model: a needs assessment model that determine needs, goals, and objectives in a deductive manner, usually starting from a preexisting but tentative list of goals of education.

Type I model: a needs assessment model that determines needs, goals, and objectives in an inductive manner, usually starting from a determination of present (or extant) behaviors.

Exercises

1.   A needs assessment is a _____ analysis.
2.   The two "polar" positions in a needs assessment are _____ _____ and _____.
3.   A needs assessment must have at least the following three characteristics:
     a.   _____
     b.   _____
     c.   _____
4.   What are the differences between a need, a want, a desire?
5.   Who are the "educational partners"?
6.   Describe the three types of needs assessment models (type I, type D, and type C).
7.   Write three examples of goal indicators that will meet the requirements of a measurable objective.
8.   Critique the following "need" statement:

We need more money for the Rendon Junior High School immediately.

9.   Prepare both a needs assessment summary table and a needs statement, including a statement of "what is" and "what should be" for each of the educational partners (learners, implementers, and society). Check to be sure each "polar" position is mentioned in measurable performance terms. Include the sources of data that go into the statements.
10.   List some tools that might be useful in conducting and completing a needs assessment for your educational agency.

mission analysis

chapter 4

The major purpose of a system analysis is to identify the requirements for problem solving and possible ways to accomplish each requirement. From a delineated problem based on documented needs, we analyze the problem to identify all the characteristics of the problem, we determine interrelations among the parts of the problem, and we specify measurable requirements for reaching the best solution for the overall problem *and* for solving each subpart of the problem.

Frequently educational problems are identified in relatively global and diffuse terms; however, an educational planner or an educational designer is required to determine the exact nature of the problem so that a precise referent is available against which further analysis, design, implementation, and evaluation may take place. For instance, an educational mission (overall job) of developing each child to his own capacity provides little usable information to a planner. What is necessary is a more precise goal statement covering the actual range of capacities and the entry characteristics of the learners and identifying the actual skills and knowledges that are required for successful completion of the mission. Specification of exactly what is to be done as a result of planned activity is usually a gritty, grinding experience the first few times it is undertaken. However, as with any other learned behavior, the associated skills improve, and each time system analysis is applied to educational planning, less time and effort are required. (Remember the first time you slipped behind the wheel of a car to learn how to drive, confronting an array of knobs, levers, and pedals? Surely this was a skill far too complex for *you* to master. In retrospect, driving was fairly simple to learn, and for the most part we now drive relatively automatically.) With practice, the skills required in system analysis will become easier and easier to use, and the results from valid educational planning should be well worth the effort.

Although the needs (gaps) may be many and varied, and although they may come from many sources, the educational problem-solving effort is most efficient and effective when legitimate high-priority problems are identified and analyzed and are based on documented needs as described in the previous chapter. It might be useful here to recall from Chapter 3 on needs assessment and from the introductory material in Chapter 2 the relationship between needs and problems. An educational need, as we define it here, is a measurable gap between our current outcomes and our desired (or required) outcomes. When we perform a needs assessment we end up with a number of gaps which are placed in priority order, and the gaps to be eliminated are stated. The gaps, once selected for action *are* the problems. Thus, problems are selected gaps (needs). If we have no gaps, then we have no problems.

What is a Mission?

A mission is an overall job—a product, a completed service, or a change in the condition of something or somebody—that must be accomplished. As we have previously said, mission analysis is a determination of "where we are going," "how we know when we have arrived," and "what the major steps are to get from here to there." Since educational planning should consistently build on acquired analytical data, the planner must be sure that the data being used are as complete, correct, and current as possible. A valid and precise base for making this first and crucial product or outcome commitment is imperative.

Mission Analysis Elements

As defined here, mission analysis consists of two elements:

1. Mission objective and associated performance requirements.
2. Mission profile.

Both of these elements are described, along with the process by which they are derived.

The Mission Objective

A mission objective is a precise statement expressed in performance terms which qualifies the outcome of a mission. The mission objective may derive from a goal relative to meeting a need. The purpose of framing a mission objective is to translate such an intent into the measurable, most general—yet inclusive—statement of the outcome (mission) that can be made. Examples of missions for an educational planner could include such directives as:

1. Build a high school.
2. Determine learner needs in the Melton school district.
3. Hire new teachers.
4. Develop an instructional media center.

Although many problems are given to us in these terms, the foregoing mandates do not contain enough information to allow planners to go to work. We have to be more explicit if we are to proceed with confidence that our effort will be efficient and effective.

Mission objectives are *performance* objectives that specify outcomes in measurable terms. They require the same degree of specificity as any other performance or behavioral objectives, such as those described by Mager (1961). Therefore, a mission objective must state precisely the following conditions for the final outcome:

1. What is to be done to demonstrate completion?
2. By whom it is to be done; that is, who will display the outcome(s)?
3. Under what conditions is the outcome to be demonstrated?
4. What criteria will be used to determine if the outcome has been achieved?

Thus mission objectives designate exactly *where* one is going and/or *what* is to be produced.[1] Look at the following hypothetical mission objectives:

Unacceptable: Design a curriculum. (This is a statement of gross intent, *not* a mission objective.)

Better: By June 30, 1978, at least 90 percent of physics learners with XYZ characteristics in the Cox School District will achieve Z performance on L criterion measure. (This objective is more specific and precise than its predecessor. It states precisely *what* is going to be done, under what conditions, and to what degree; therefore, it better meets the requirements for a mission objective.)

In performing a mission analysis, then, we start by specifying what has to be done: the statement of the mission is the first step. Some examples of starting points might be:

1. *When using a full system approach model, the needs assessment data will directly provide the mission objective and performance requirements in the "what should be" statement.*

1. Get a man on Mars and retrieve him, unharmed, before 1990.

2. Reduce reported traffic accidents in California by 15 percent next year.

3. Eliminate illiteracy in Janice County within five years.

Notice that each of the foregoing statements has both quantitative and qualitative aspects. Let us break down the first illustration:

What is to be done?	Get to Mars.
By whom?	A man.
Under what condition?	By 1990, with a budget of $X.
What criteria (how much or how well)?	Return trip, 100 percent, and unharmed.

In order to assure communication, the terms and performance criteria used in a mission objective must be understood by all who will deal with that objective and its accomplishment; thus these items must also include the basis for evaluation. Since loose or nebulous terms such as *appreciate* and *feel* are not meaningful unless they are defined operationally, every effort must be made to eliminate areas of misconception or misinterpretation.

The last characteristic of a mission objective, which is more closely related to curriculum objectives than to managerial and administrative objectives, is the requirement to "focus on the learner."

There are, then, four conditions stated in a useful mission objective and together they must show at least three characteristics:

Conditions	*Characteristics*
1. What is to be done to demonstrate completion?	Objectives must communicate successfully to all users and evaluators. All of the conditions for results and must contain the basis for evaluation; they must focus on the learner, and they must be in measurable performance terms which are valid and should leave no room for confusion.
2. By whom it is to be done?	
3. Under what conditions it is to be done?	
4. What criteria will be used to determine if it is done? (How much or how well is it to be done?)	

Let us identify a hypothetical mission and "walk it through" as a planner might do in deriving an adequately stated mission objective.

We might begin with a statement of the mission (i.e., what we want to accomplish), revising and refining this statement of intent until it has evolved to a measurable performance objective.

1. "Improve California education."

We must refine this gross statement until it is more precise, ultimately relating to reducing or eliminating a defined and documented need.

2. "Increase California student mastery of critical skill and knowledge areas and improve self-concept of learners."
The planner has refined further—by specifying the fundamental critical skills and knowledge areas that also *might* be associated with how a student perceives himself.

Continuing:

3. "Measurably improve California in-school student mastery in reading and arithmetic, and produce an increase in self-concept of learners."
The planner has moved closer to measurability.

Continuing:

4. "Increase California in-school student performance as measured by X valid reading test and Z valid arithmetic test by 10 and 12 percent mean improvements, respectively, and improve learner self-concept significantly among these learners as measured by Q valid instrument within two years."

Statement 1 has been transformed into an acceptable objective by supplying performance criteria and the bases for evaluation. As we become more precise, we derive a mission objective that is realistic and assessable and, moreover, communicates the product or outcome precisely with virtually no margin for misinterpretation.

Performance Requirements

It should be apparent that precise, measurable criteria for describing and determining outcomes form a critical element in the statement of a mission objective. These criteria are termed *performance requirements.*

The ultimate result of the accomplishment of a mission is the creation of a product or the achievement of a specific, measurable outcome. Performance requirements for the mission provide the exact specifications by which success (or failure) of the mission may be measured. They include the following:

1. Specifications stating the criteria by which the terminal success of the mission objective may be measured—what the product will look like or actually do.
2. Specifications stating the context or "ground rules" under which the product is to be produced, such as environment, costs, personnel, and other "givens."

Performance Requirement Defined

A performance requirement is comprised of the measurable criteria that describe the product of the mission or the outcome from performing a function. They may include such categories as how the product is to perform, the conditions under which it is to perform, product design characteristics, and performance specifications and restrictions or rules placed on the development of the product. They specify what the product will look like and/or do, and the "given" conditions for its development, if any. An example for the specifications of a hypothetical self-instructional program might be the following:

1. There must be learner achievement with the program to the criterion level of 90/90 (90 percent of learners with score 90 percent or better on the criterion test) when the resulting curriculum package is used by the specified target population and the test items are related to the defined needs.

2. The curriculum package (program) must not cost more than $4.25.

3. Eighty-five percent of all learners using the package will complete it to mastery within two hours.

4. Two of the five school board members are opposed to this project.

Performance requirements are frequently set by the "client" (we all have at least one boss). They represent the client's (or boss's) perceptions of what must be done, and thus his notions of how evaluation of success or failure will be made. A client may state requirements in non-assessable terms. If we act on these, we take a risk of misinterpreting what he wants and actually accomplishing something quite different from what was expected. Mission analysis represents a process by which (1) client and planner may arrive at a set of measurable criteria for expected outcomes when the mission is accomplished or (2) the planner may "renegotiate" the mission with the client if it develops that the original intent is not sufficiently functional.

There is another important point to consider. Just because a client has established a performance requirement, it does not necessarily follow that the requirement is realistic or even feasible. The educational planner using the tools and following the steps of system analysis will have to evaluate the feasibility of requirements that are given. When stated in precise, objective, measurable terms, the performance requirements will provide the criteria for the early determination of the feasibility of accomplishing that which has been requested. (More about determining feasibility is presented in Chapter 7, Methods–Means Analysis.)

Listing of performance requirements: When performance requirements are being identified, we will want to keep track of them, and this is best done in tabular form, associating with each performance requirement, by the number of the function, a written statement of that performance requirement (Table 4.1).

TABLE 4.1 Performance Requirements

Function and Number	Associated Performance Requirement
1.1 xxxxxxxxxxx xxxxxxx xx xxxxxxx xx	xxxxxxxxxxxxxxxxx xxxxxxxxxxx xxxxxxxxxxxxxxx
1.2 xxxxxx xxx x	same as 1.0
1.3 xxxx x xxxxx	xxxxxxxxxxxxxxxxx
1.4 xx xx x xxx	same as 0.0[a] and 1.3

[a]0.0 is the symbol used for the mission objective and performance requirements. There does not have to be a new performance requirement for each function if the performance requirement from a previous function is appropriate—it should then only be referenced (such as "same as 0.0").

As the system analysis identifies more and more functions, the analyst will be keeping recording performance requirements that are associated with the functions and tasks which will require several pages for a complete analysis. When a performance requirement is the same for one function as it is for another (or the same as that stated in the mission objective and its performance requirements) it is *not* necessary to list the performance requirements over again—simply note that it is the same (as in Table 4.1).

Obstacles

As potential obstacles are identified in the mission analysis, they become performance requirements; that is, they provide criteria for specifying the characteristics or the conditions under which the outcome of the mission must be accomplished. If, for instance, it is given that "no additional funds may be spent over and above that which is already budgeted," then this factor becomes one of the ground rules. Even if a performance requirement is unachievable (i.e., a constraint exists), the unfavorable requirement must be specified and an attempt must be made to meet it before aborting or changing the mission. Thus we see that a constraint arises when it appears that a mission objective, a performance requirement, or a set of performance requirements is not achievable. (The determination of a constraint condition is discussed in Chapter 7.)

A constraint is resolvable in several ways. *First*, it may be possible to change the mission objective and/or the performance requirements; if a requirement for something no longer exists, then the constraint is operationally removed. A *second* possibility is to reconcile the constraint by creating a new or different way to meet the requirement, and thus, to remove the constraint operationally. A *third* possibility is to reach a "compromise" relative to the performance requirement and its achievement. This compromise might be said to amount to bringing an out-of-bounds condition into tolerance. This reconciliation of a constraint might be exemplified by the easing of a specification that had been set for an objective (e.g., changing a performance requirement of "a mean of 75 with a standard deviation of 12" to "a mean of 75 with a standard deviation of 15"). In this example, the basic requirement remains, but there is a variation granted in the "spread" in the student's performance. A *fourth* possibility for dealing with a constraint is to stop—if you can't get there from here, why go further?

The identification of a constraint[2] requires decisions to (1) invent, innovate, or create, (2) renegotiate or (3) *STOP* (it just would not make sense to proceed with a problem if there are positive indications that the effort would be a failure). When we have identified a constraint, we know what would result in a higher-than-acceptable probability of failure.

Putting Specificity into a Mission Objective

In Chapter 3 it was noted that an assessment of educational needs would provide hard data concerning problem dimension of "what is" and "what is required." Hard empirical data indicate that measurable criteria have been identified to document both the beginning and the end characteristics of a given problem area.

The job of writing a mission objective and its associated performance requirements without hard data from a needs assessment obliges the educational planner to obtain valid data on the problem and the characteristics that will allow the determination of the relative success or failure of the mission. This additional job for the planner or designer is vital to the success of the educational system planning effort. Referring to Mager (1961), "If you don't know where you are going, you might end up someplace else."

One may set objectives in precise measurable terms only to find that precision does not assure validity; however further assurance of validity is furnished by the needs assessment data. Also, planners may find it difficult to get from a general statement of a mission intent to the detailed performance requirements involved in completing a useful mission analysis. In this instance, consider the possible usefulness of a conceptual pyramid (Fig. 4.1) where the analysis proceeds from gross objectives to a

---

2. *Constraints and their reconciliation are more fully discussed in Chapter 7. Their importance is best understood when the idea is related to the methods–means analysis.*

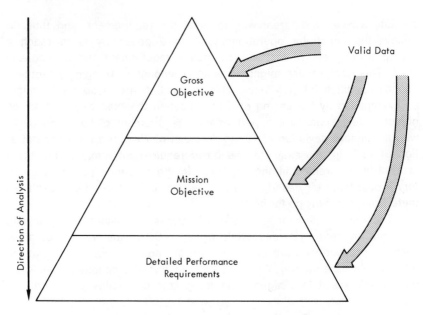

FIG. 4.1.   A possible process for deriving relevant and detailed mission objectives and their associated performance requirements.

mission objective and then to the detailed performance requirements to describe the characteristics of the outcome of the mission. This is a gradual process for achieving increasing specificity and precision while moving from the general to the specific.

Viewed in this manner, the mission objective and its associated performance requirements actually form a unitary package that states what is to be done and how one can determine when the job has been completed. Without the performance requirements attached, a mission objective seldom supplies the criterion for evaluation and thus will not give the educational planner the information required to derive a relevant and practical plan for achieving the objective and its associated performance requirements. Together, then, the mission objective and the performance requirements provide the starting referent and the specifications for system analysis.

The Mission Profile

The second element of mission analysis is the *mission profile*. The planning effort so far has yielded (1) *what* is to be done, (the mission objective) and (2) the *performance requirements* for the mission.

The planner now must address himself to proceeding from where he is to where he should be. This involves *what* is to be done, not *"how"* and not *"who will do it."* The "things" that must be done to accomplish the overall job regardless of how it gets done are termed *functions.* When the major functions of a mission are identified and placed in logical sequence, they constitute the *mission profile*—a management plan identifying the outcomes that must be completed to accomplish a mission. Thus the mission profile represents the central path for achievement of the end product. The discrete functions within the mission profile may number from two to *N* functions, depending on the complexity of the mission.

Using a Discrepancy Analysis in Preparing the Mission Profile

In an earlier discussion, it was noted that the identification of needs constituted a part of the needs assessment (or discrepancy analysis). This notion of a discrepancy analysis appears continuously as part of system analysis, for in several instances we want to identify what is to be done to eliminate a discrepancy (i.e., to meet a need).

In mission analysis, we have identified "where we should be," formulating this body of data as the mission objective and the performance requirements. Now we must plan the path for getting from our current position to our required position, and we should derive the mission profile— a management plan identifying *what* is to be done to get us from the "what is" area of our needs assessment statement to "what should be," as stated in our mission objective and performance requirements. In other words, the mission profile is a statement of functions that, performed in their proper order, will eliminate the discrepancy identified in our first and most significant discrepancy analysis, the needs assessment.

How Is a Mission Profile Derived?

Step 1:   Obtain the mission objective and the performance requirements that tell where we will be when we have completed the mission. Next describe the status quo. A mission profile, as we know, is derived to identify what is to be done to get us from "what is" to "what is required." Now list the necessary functions (or outcomes, or subproducts). In this type of analysis, the planner must decide on the logical order of functions to be performed.[3] Be sure to leave out *how* the job will be done.

3. *In performing a system analysis, the planner may, if he prefers, reverse this normal chronological process and move from the end to the beginning. In this "back-to-front mode" the mission objective defines the end; it states where you will be when you have accomplished the mission, and this becomes a "known." Then the analyst begins with the "known" and works backward until he arrives at the initial state.*

Step 2: When the first major function in the mission profile has been identified, the question is then asked, "What is the next logical step to take?" The next function is then identified and listed. This process is continued until it is ascertained that one has moved from the *first* function of the mission profile to the *last* function required to achieve the mission objective and its performance requirements.

Step 3: When all the major functions in the mission profile have been identified, they are reexamined against the needs, the mission objective, and the performance requirements in order to assure internal consistency among the functions and external validity based on the needs.

It should be emphasized that the process of check and recheck is performed throughout the entire analysis process. It is necessary to review the scope and order of identified functions to determine whether any have been omitted or if unnecessary ones are included, and to assure that they are in proper sequence. Some functions may be best unified under a larger function, for example, and these should be identified in a collective manner. Examination of the mission profile may also uncover performance requirements that were previously unidentified or overlooked.

Step 4: Once internal consistency has been determined, arrange the functions in an orderly array of rectangles or squares and connect the graphic "blocks" with a solid line so that the arrow points follow the flow of the functions from the first to the last.[4]

As the analysis process proceeds, there may come to light new data, which in turn might alter the mission profile. System analysis is a dynamic process and, through the utilization of newly uncovered data, the mission objective, the performance requirements, and/or the mission profile might be subject to change. *The analyst must be ready and willing to change the profile at any time*—it should be "cast in wax," not in concrete!

The overall process involved in a mission analysis is shown in Fig. 4.2 in the form of a mission profile. The major functions appear as described in this chapter, and the relations among the various functions are made clear. These functions are: (1.0) state the mission objective, then (2.0) state the performance requirements in measurable terms which derive from the mission objective, (3.0) derive the management plan which shows the major functions required to accomplish the mission—the mission profile, and (4.0) revise any or all of the previous steps as required to maintain consistency between the original requirement and the steps and subproducts derived in performing a mission analysis. Not all the steps discussed in this chapter are shown in Figure 4.2; these represent

---

4. *More detailed information concerning flow chart preparation may be found in Chapter 5, Function Analysis.*

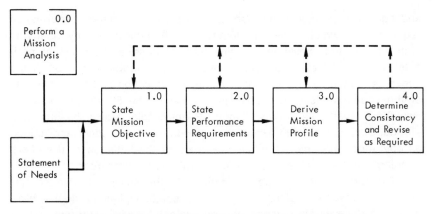

FIG. 4.2. A sample mission profile for accomplishing the mission of "perform a mission analysis." This example shows that there are four basis functions or steps that may be involved in performing a mission analysis. Note that revision of any previous function is possible; the dotted lines show feedback of data for the purpose of revision.

subordinate functions to be performed and constitute subfunctions, which are taken up in greater detail in the next chapter. Notice that the mission profile constitutes a management plan (or road map) in that it sets forth the major functions involved in getting from "what is" to "what is required."

A hypothetical mission analysis might be taken from a work entitled "An Exercise in the Analysis of Planned Change in Education" [Kaufman and Corrigan (1967)]. Here, for the sake of explanation of the steps and tools of system analysis, a rather staggering hypothetical problem was tackled. Fig. 4.3 represents a possible mission profile for the tentative

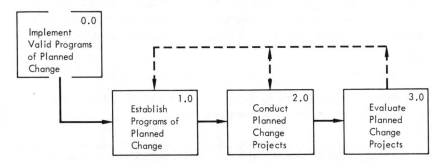

FIG. 4.3. A hypothetical mission profile for implementing valid programs of planned change in education. After Kaufman and Corrigan (1967).

and equally hypothetical mission objective and associated performance requirements, which were to identify the 50 highest priority needs in education, identify possible cost-effective solutions, and implement projects to reduce or eliminate each need with measurable reduction in the needs as judged by (1) the commissioner of education and (2) at least 35 of the superintendents of public instruction of the 50 states, including New York, California, Texas, Illinois, Pennsylvania, Massachusetts, and Florida. Such measurable reduction in needs must be evident and judged as operating satisfactorily within five years of the initiation of the effort. Funding is to be obtained from both federal and local sources.

The three major functions identified in the mission profile are (1) establish programs of planned change, (2) conduct planned change projects, and (3) evaluate planned change projects. Revision throughout the project and at the completion of the third function in the mission profile is indicated by the dotted line, denoting the availability of performance data for revision to any or all previous functions and tasks.

It should be emphasized that not all mission profiles look alike. Recall the basic six-step problem-solving model which shows a mission profile for identifying and solving problems logically, and review the mission profile presented in Chapter 2 and indicating the functions to be performed in designing instructional materials using a system approach (Fig. 2.2, p. 16). Fig. 4.4, (pages 66-71) for instance, is a mission profile developed for a K-12 program for Mexican–American youth in a rural area.[5] Fig. 4.5 shows a mission profile for individualizing an instruction program.[6] Here the gross objective is to develop method and means that, if implemented, would change individual student behavior in a specified manner as defined by documented needs (individually responsive instruction).

Each function in a mission profile identifies a subproduct—an outcome required for the partial fulfillment of the mission objective and its performance requirements. The total of the subproducts identified in a mission profile will yield the larger, overall product specified in the mission objective and its performance requirements. (Formation of flow charts such as mission profiles is detailed in the next chapter.)

Summary

A mission is the statement of intent about the overall job we want to do, and it should be based on documented needs.

5. *The material relating to this project is reproduced with the permission of the WASCO Union School District. It was developed with funding from the U.S. Office of Education under ESEA Title III.*

6. *The material relating to this project is reproduced with the permission of the Utah System Approach to Individualized Learning (U-SAIL) funded by the U.S. Office of Education under ESEA Title III.*

A mission objective presents the mission precisely as a performance specification, stating *what* is to be accomplished, by whom, and under what conditions; the degree to which the mission is to be accomplished is also specified.

The performance requirements specify measurable products (or outcomes) of the mission and set forth the specifications within which the product of the mission must be achieved. Together, the mission objective and the performance requirements state "where we are going and how we know when we have arrived."

In a logically ordered sequence, the mission profile identifies all the major functions that must be performed to achieve the mission and produce the product (outcome) satisfying the specifications contained in the performance requirements. This is the central path for meeting the mission objective. With the completion of the mission objective, its performance requirements, and the mission profile, the educational planner has completed the mission analysis. Now the stage is set for the second phase of system analysis, namely, function analysis.

The following steps are involved in performing a mission analysis:

1. Obtain needs data from needs assessment and the problem statements that derived from the assessment.

2. Derive the mission objective and the performance requirements so that it is possible to answer in measurable performance terms the following questions: (1) what is to be done to demonstrate completion? (2) by whom it is to be demonstrated? (3) under what conditions is it to be demonstrated? and (4) what criteria will be used to determine if it has been done? These statements of "where we are going" and "how we know when we have arrived" form the mission objective *and* the performance requirements.

3. Verify that the mission objective and the performance requirements accurately represent the problem selected based on the documented needs. If not, reconcile the discrepancy based on the needs data.

4. Prepare the mission profile, which shows the major functions required to get from "what is" to "what should be" as stated in the discrepancy analysis (needs assessment). Remember that the mission profile is a management plan setting forth the functions necessary to eliminate the discrepancy that constitutes the problem. Each function identified will:

a. Be stated in action terms and identify an outcome (or subproduct) that is to be accomplished.

b. Be graphically positioned to show its relative independence from the other functions in the mission profile.

c. Be numbered in sequence to show the relation between each function and every other function.

d. Be joined by solid lines with arrows to denote the exact flow and the relation between each function and all the other functions.

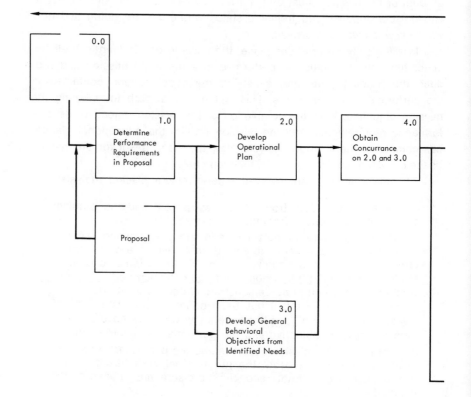

FIG. 4.4. An example of a mission profile developed for a comprehensive educational program for Mexican–American learners. Developed by Robert Kane, Roger A. Kaufman, Jack Ward, and Raul J. Hernandez, in connection with the Wasco Union School District's Mexican-American Research Project, "A Gestalt Approach to Developing the Bi-lingual, Bi-cultural Resources of the Mexican-American."

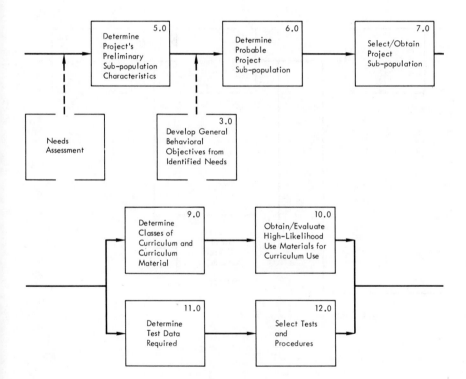

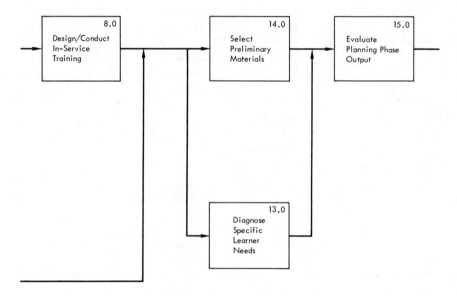

FIG. 4.4. Cont.

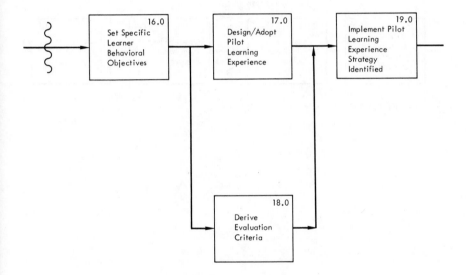

Phase I – Pilot

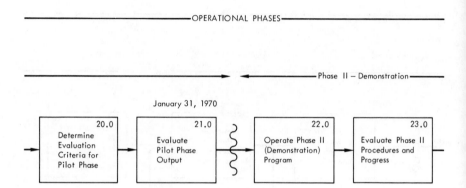

FIG. 4.4 Cont.

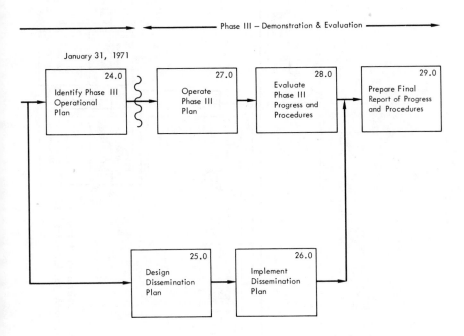

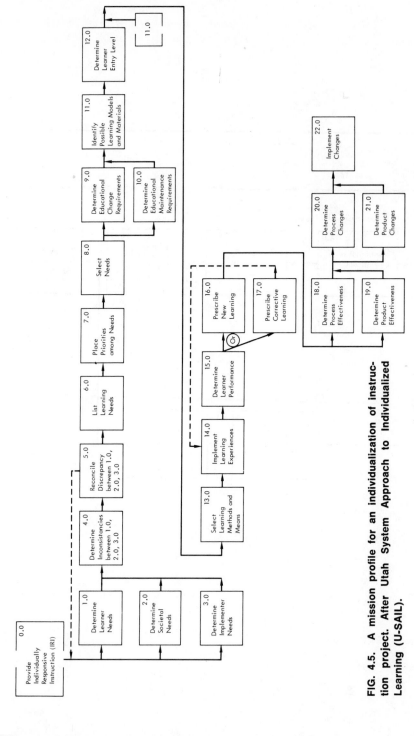

FIG. 4.5. A mission profile for an individualization of instruction project. After Utah System Approach to Individualized Learning (U-SAIL).

5. Check the mission analysis to make sure that all elements are presented, that they are in the correct order, that they are consistent with the mission objective and the performance requirements, and that they are consistent with the needs assessment and problem statements. Make any necessary changes based on the needs assessment data.

Glossary

Mission: the overall job to be done to meet the identified and documented needs.

Mission objective: an objective that measurably states the specifications for determining when we have successfully reached where we should be. This performance objective has four elements. (1) what is to be done to demonstrate completion? (2) by whom it is to be demonstrated? (3) under what conditions it is to be demonstrated, and (4) what criteria will be used to determine if it has been done?

Mission profile: a management plan depicting, in flow chart form, the functions or elements necessary to get from where one is to the satisfactory completion of the mission (as measured by the mission objective and its associated performance requirements).

Exercises

Produce a mission objective, performance requirements, and a mission profile for an educational problem of your choice which will meet all of the criteria for these elements:

1. What is to be done to demonstrate completion of the mission?

2. By whom it is to be demonstrated?

3. Under what conditions it is to be demonstrated?

4. What criteria will be used to determine if it has been done?

This four-part mission objective will state the exact outcome of the mission and contain the criterion basis for evaluation; in the case of curriculum design, the mission must be learner oriented.

Performance requirements will contain product specifications, restrictions, and performance characteristics of the product (where applicable) and will identify measurement criteria.

The mission profile will identify the major functions to be performed in order to successfully accomplish the mission. Each function must appear in its logical order. The mission profile must be internally consistent with the mission objective and the performance requirements; if implemented, it should result in the achievement of the stated mission objective and performance requirements.

Answer correctly at least 11 of the following items, including the answers to questions 1, 2, 4, 5, 7, 9, and 10.

Fill in the Blanks

1. A mission objective must fulfill the following three requirements:

   a. _____

   b. _____

   c. (for curriculum design): _____

2. We call the description of the product of the mission, its specification, tolerances, characteristics, and restrictions—generally "givens" by the client—the _____. These tell what the product must _____ and/or _____ _____.

3. The mission profile is a sequence of _____ representing the major milestones that must be passed to accomplish the mission. It is considered to be the _____ to mission achievement.

4. Before the mission profile can be derived, the _____ _____ and _____ must be identified.

Answer the Following Questions

5. What is the role of the mission objective?

6. What is the role of the performance requirements?

7. State how the mission objective, performance requirements, and mission profile relate to one another and collectively in what order they are derived and why this order must be maintained.

8. What is the relation between the mission analysis and what is to follow in a complete system analysis?

9. Design a criterion measure for the performance objective on page 56 that would test the performance of the learner in terms of the stated objective.

10. Write ten objective test questions that would test the relevant concepts in the mission analysis chapter.

function analysis

chapter 5

A function is one of several related outcomes contributing to a larger outcome. A function is usually a collection of required jobs or tasks necessary to achieve a specified objective or bring about a given product or outcome.

In the chapter on *mission analysis*, we stated that a mission objective specified the *what* that was to be accomplished. Referring to the definition of a function, one may see that analysis is the process used to determine what functions or jobs must be done to accomplish the mission objective. Functions, then, are things that have to be done to achieve a product or part of a total product. Some examples of functions as they might be stated in a function analysis are:

Perform function analysis.
Complete district budget.
Hire teachers.
Collect data.
Summarize data.

In performing a function analysis, the system planner is further extending the planning that began with the needs assessment, the mission objective, the performance requirements, and the mission profile. At the same time, he is deriving and identifying additional "whats" that have to be dealt with in order to assure the successful achievement of the mission objective and performance requirements. Notice that in this phase, as in all system analysis, the concern is only with the "whats" and not the "hows." As with mission analysis, the analyst is identifying *what* has to be done as well as the *order* in which the operations are to be performed.

Function analysis proceeds from the top-level (mission profile) functions, one at a time, in an orderly manner. The product of any function analysis is the identification of an array of functions and subfunctions (down to the lowest level of relevance), including the determination of the interrelations required to achieve a mission. Examine the following hypothetical situation.

Need: Z percent of California school graduates earn F percent less than a subsistence wage, and this Z percent should earn a subsistence wage or better.

Problem: Provide for the Z percent so that 95 percent of these will earn at least a subsistence wage.

Solution: Improve reading skills by using the "X" method of reading content improvement.

Critique: The solution is proposed before an analysis has been performed to determine requirements and functions. Problem solving jumped from the problem to "how" without determining the "whats."

Function analysis proceeds from the results of the mission analysis to a precise statement naming the functions that must be performed in order to solve the problem.

Need: "Q percent" of third graders in the Wood School District read below "P" level, and this Q percent should read at the "P" level or better.

Problem: By June 1, reading skills of third graders in the Wood School District will be at the "P" level or better.

Functions: Determine present reading skill and subskill areas; determine teaching/reading training resources; etc.

Note that the function analysis process (1) analyzes what should be done and (2) gives the proper order of jobs, with the goal of achieving the mission objective (and thus solving the problem):

It analyzes.
It identifies.
It orders.

Levels of Function Analysis

It was mentioned previously that functions and related subfunctions are identified through the process of function analysis. Recalling the definition of a function as one of a group of outcomes (or products) contributing to a larger action (or product), a key to the levels of function analysis may be found in the words "larger action" (or product). Larger products (or actions) may be referred to as *higher level functions*. The highest level function is the mission, and all other functions derive from that highest level or overall function.

One useful way of viewing the relation between mission analysis and function analysis is in terms of a matrix, with the mission analysis forming the "top" of the matrix and the function analysis as the "depth" dimension. In performing a function analysis, we are filling in the "depth" or additional dimensions of the mission analysis. Greatly simplified, such a matrix would resemble Fig. 5.1. The function analysis is a vertical expansion of the mission analysis—each element in the mission profile is composed of functions, and it is the role of the function analyst to identify, for each function named in the mission analysis and depicted in the mission profile, all the subfunctions and their interrelations. This vertical expansion might be further conceptualized by the model of Fig. 5.2.

The function analysis, then, is filling in the detail, including the specification of requirements and interrelations among the identified subfunctions, for each element in the mission profile. As we note later in this chapter, there is an additional manner for the identification of the ways in which the subfunctions interrelate with other subfunctions. When there are interrelations between different major functions identified in the mission profile—or with their subfunctions, these interrelations are called interactions. Because a successful system has many parts (or subsystems) which must work together, a critical part of system analysis is concerned with identifying interactions and planning for successful meshing of parts.

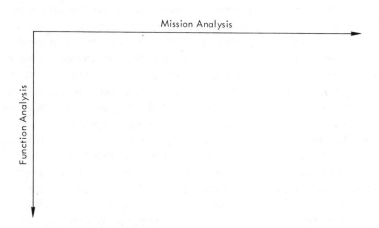

FIG. 5.1. Function analysis may be seen as a vertical expansion of the mission analysis.

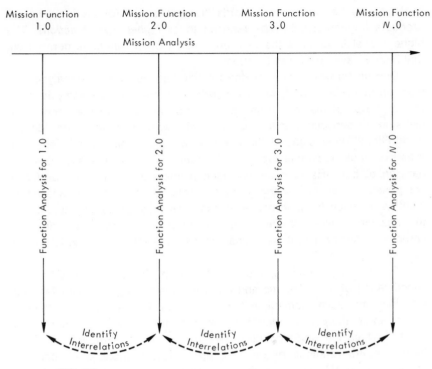

FIG. 5.2.

"Smaller" contributing outcomes are called lower-level functions or subfunctions. The analyst looks at the higher-level functions (beginning with the functions identified in the mission profile) in much the same manner as he would use a microscope with varying degrees of magnification power to examine a natural phenomenon (Corrigan and Kaufman, 1966). A low magnification power would show a larger field, and a higher magnification power would show a small field but with more detail.

In using this analysis "microscope," the planner attempts to keep the analysis at one particular *level* at any given time. He attends first to the identification of the overall functions (or higher-level functions), thereafter focusing at the *same level of magnitude* until all functions of equal magnitude have been identified. Since the mission profile represents the primary functions which, when accomplished, will yield the product specified in the mission objective, the mission profile level is called the top level. The planner then uses a "higher power of magnification" and analyzes each high-level function to identify the subfunctions which collectively would accomplish each top-level function. Only when he is satisfied that he has identified all the subfunctions and that they are internally consistent with all the previous steps does he proceed to lower levels.

To understand levels of function analysis, consider a map of the United States, where the highest level to be analyzed would be the whole country; the next level, the states; a still lower level, the counties; and perhaps the lowest level, the cities and towns. (If one required more detailed information, the cities and towns could be further broken down into districts, neighborhoods, blocks, residences, buildings, parking lots and parks, etc.) In performing a function analysis by levels, the analyst makes every attempt not to confuse counties with states, or cities with counties. States functions are kept at the "state" level of analysis, and counties functions are kept with "county" functions.

A function, as we know, is something to be achieved or done. For example: Provide learners with function analysis skills. To identify the function as discrete, and to show its relation to other functions that might be identified, we put it in a numbered box:

```
┌─────────────────────┐
│           1.0       │
│                     │
│  Provide Learners   │
│  with               │
│  Function Analysis  │
│  Skills             │
│                     │
└─────────────────────┘
```

We have derived "provide learners with function analysis skills" (or block 1.0) from a hypothetical needs assessment and mission analysis. It should be noted that it is the first of several prime functions in this hypothetical mission profile, so we call this prime function a top-level function. Consider the two following examples:

A.

```
┌─────────────────────┐
│           1.0       │
│  Function Analysis  │
│                     │
│                     │
│                     │
│                     │
│                     │
└─────────────────────┘
```

B.

```
┌─────────────────────┐
│           1.0       │
│  Provide Learners   │
│  with               │
│  Function Analysis  │
│  Skills             │
│                     │
└─────────────────────┘
```

Box *A* does not tell what is to be accomplished; it could be interpreted as "read about" or even "ignore" the stated function. Function shows a product (or subproduct) to be achieved and as such is really a "miniature" mission objective with the same properties and character-

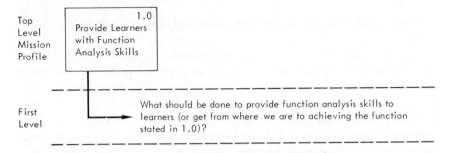

FIG. 5.3. "Breaking-out" or expanding a top-level function.

istics. Box *B*, of course, is a properly stated top-level function, revealing what has to be done.

The next step in demonstrating this hypothetical function analysis is to analyze the functions necessary to provide learners with function analysis skills. This requires the analyst to "drop" to a first level below the top (or mission profile level) function; in other words perform a vertical expansion[1] (see Fig. 5.3).

It is possible to keep analyzing "lower-level" functions that are necessary to perform higher-level functions until there are a number of "layers" or levels in the function analysis.[2] Fig. 5.4 illustrates the numbering format

1. Such a "dropping down" and expanding is sometimes referred to as "breaking-out" a function.
2. Only the analysis of function 1.0 is shown and then only to the second level. In actual performance, all top-level functions are analyzed to as many levels as required.

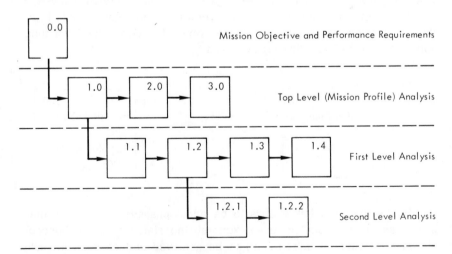

FIG. 5.4. A hypothetical expansion.

only. In actual function analysis, each function block would contain the statement of the function *and* the appropriate reference number. Since the overall function is the mission objective, it is called 0.0 in a flow diagram.

The Rules of Function Analysis

The rules of function analysis are not designed to make the process difficult, but to:

1. Facilitate keeping track of where one is and show requirements for getting to where one should be.
2. Allow communication with others.

Rule 1:   All blocks are square *or* rectangular.

Rule 2:   Each block contains a verb.

Rule 3:   Function blocks are consistently connected as in Fig. 5.5.

To see if it works, see Fig. 5.6.

Rule 4:   A decimal system is used in numbering, and a decimal point and a number are added for each level analyzed (Fig. 5.7).

Rule 5:   If a higher level function cannot be broken down into two or more functions, don't break it down.

When you have done a function analysis, drawing function blocks and connecting them according to the rules, you have prepared a *function flow block diagram.*

A function flow block diagram graphically reveals the order, stages, and interrelationships of *"what"* has to be accomplished. Done properly, a function analysis will identify and display:

1. What has to be done?
2. In what order must it be done?
3. What component functions compose each higher-level function?
4. What are the relations between the functions?

A function analysis for performing a function analysis might be set up as in Fig. 5.8.

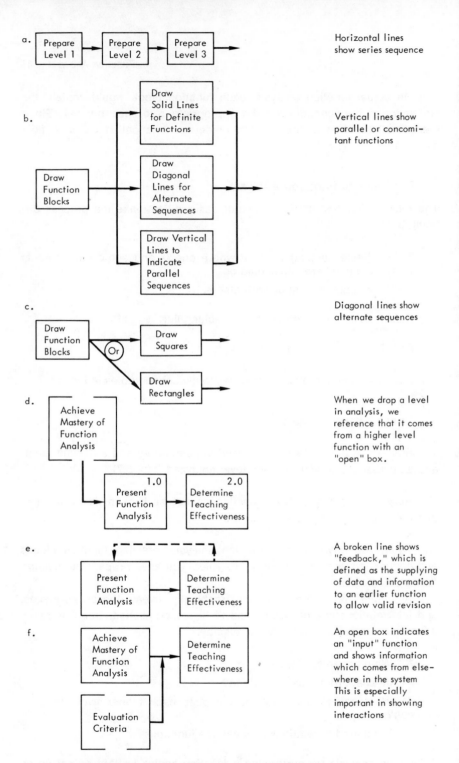

a.

| Prepare Level 1 | → | Prepare Level 2 | → | Prepare Level 3 | → |

Horizontal lines show series sequence

b.

Draw Function Blocks →

Draw Solid Lines for Definite Functions

Draw Diagonal Lines for Alternate Sequences

Draw Vertical Lines to Indicate Parallel Sequences

Vertical lines show parallel or concomitant functions

c.

Draw Function Blocks (Or) → Draw Squares

Draw Rectangles

Diagonal lines show alternate sequences

d.

Achieve Mastery of Function Analysis

1.0 Present Function Analysis → 2.0 Determine Teaching Effectiveness

When we drop a level in analysis, we reference that it comes from a higher level function with an "open" box.

e.

Present Function Analysis → Determine Teaching Effectiveness

A broken line shows "feedback," which is defined as the supplying of data and information to an earlier function to allow valid revision

f.

Achieve Mastery of Function Analysis → Determine Teaching Effectiveness

Evaluation Criteria

An open box indicates an "input" function and shows information which comes from elsewhere in the system This is especially important in showing interactions

FIG. 5.5. Some formulating conventions for system analysis flow charts.

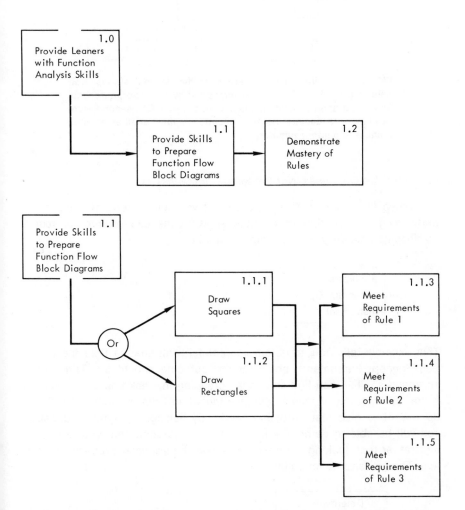

FIG. 5.6. Some flow charting rules depicted in flow chart format.

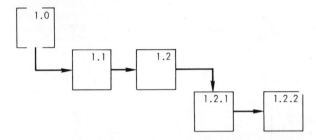

**FIG. 5.7. 1.0: top level (a zero after the decimal always indi-
cates top level); 1.X: first level (identified by a number, a decimal
point, and another number other than zero); 1.X.Y: second level
(a number, a decimal point, a second number, another decimal
point, and another number).**

Functions Are Outcomes, Not Processes or Means

When first performing a function analysis, one often lists means for
performing the function rather than showing the end product or result.
For instance, an *erroneous* example might be:

```
Administer the
Jones Self-Concept
Instrument
```

This example tells *how* to obtain self-concept information (use the Jones
Self-Concept Instrument), not what the outcome should be. Throughout
an analysis, when you find solutions "creeping in," ask yourself, "What is
it that this method or means will give me when I am through?" Or, "Why
do I want to give that particular test?" By asking this type of question
you will be able to determine the product or outcome that you are seeking, rather than locking yourself into a less-than-optimal process or solution. Thus a better function is:

```
Determine
Individual
Self-Concept
```

One of the critical results of performing a system analysis in general
and a function analysis in particular is that we are seeking to free our-
selves from the possible "strait-jackets" of the past with new and better
ways of doing things.

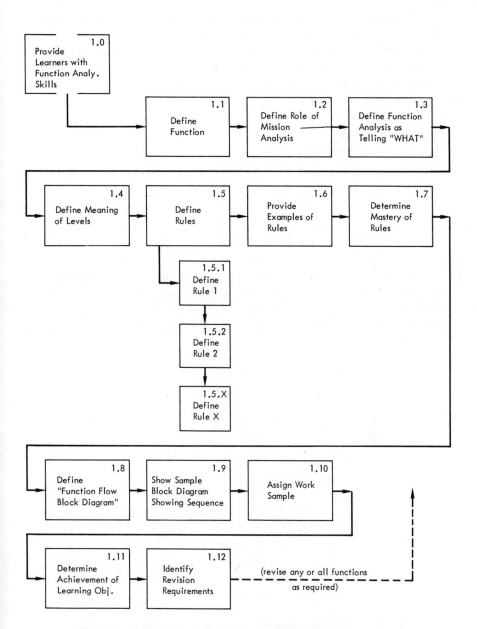

FIG. 5.8. A flow chart showing a possible "break-out" of a top-level function.

Every Level of System Analysis is Related to Every Other Level

The process of system analysis really starts with the assessment of needs where discrepancies between "what is" and "what is required" are identified. The latter dimension provides the basis (or core) for the mission objective, thus furnishing the connection or "bridge" between needs assessment and mission analysis:

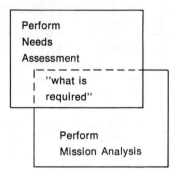

The mission analysis identifies the mission objective, the performance requirements and the mission profile, and the levels of analysis are interrelated in a logical, internally consistent manner. The mission profile (the top level of function analysis) thus bridges mission analysis and function analysis:

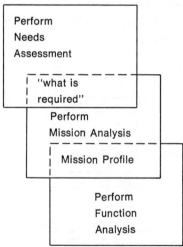

A Few Tips on Conducting an Analysis

Analysis is the process of breaking things down into their component parts and noting the interrelations between the parts.

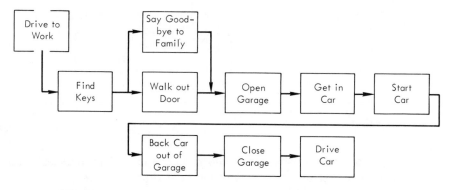

FIG. 5.9.

Analyzing a Problem

Try *listing* constituent components during analysis. For instance, in order to drive to work, you must eventually perform all the following activities:

Open garage.
Walk out door.
Start car.
Find car keys.
Drive car.

Now list the components in the order in which they would logically occur (find keys, walk out door, etc.). Scan your list critically, asking, "What have I missed?" (How about: back car out of garage, say goodbye to family, close garage door, get in car.)

Keep an open mind and be willing and ready to revise. Fig. 5.9 illustrates how the drive-to-work function may be diagrammed; note that two or more simultaneous functions may be shown in "parallel."

Determining Analysis Levels

Keep the analysis within its own level. For example, not all the components listed below are true constituents of the go-to-work function:

Get dressed.
Shine shoes.
Brush teeth.
Eat breakfast.
Drive to work.

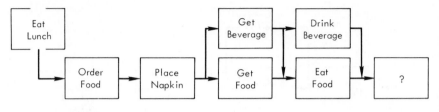

FIG. 5.10.

(Shining shoes and brushing teeth are components of "get dressed" and would be analyzed as being part of the "get dressed" level.)

In setting up practice function analyses, try to find one more component that may have been omitted. It is easy to complete Fig. 5.10. Keep drawing blocks for components—even if you don't know what they will contain—surprisingly often you will think of something. Constantly ask yourself "why?" or "what else?" Question everything. If it isn't right, make it right!

Performing a Function Analysis

The following procedure is suggested for performing a function analysis:

A. The function analysis proceeds from the mission analysis. Below is an example of a *hypothetical* mission analysis which is the starting point for the function analysis.[3]

Mission Objective:

Identify all the "creatively gifted" students in Carron High School by September 1, 1976, and increase their concept formation ability significantly (.05 level of confidence or better) as measured by the valid Rudolph Inquiry Inventory.

Performance Requirements

1. The identified students must meet the minimum standards set by the state for any program funding.

2. The name of each student identified must be accompanied by a written justification based on established criteria.

3. Project must be completed in one school year.

4. Budget is $8,000, excluding school personnel available.

5. Personnel available are:
   a.   one psychometrist (M.A.) in District employ

3. This example is a modification of an exercise prepared by Donald Goodwin and used in OPERATION PEP training and in the Chapman College Experienced Teacher Fellowship Program.

   b.   one teacher in school writing master's thesis on characteristics of creatively gifted children.
   6.   Total enrollment is 2000.
   7.   Access to cumulative records is available to authorized personnel only.
   8.   Maximum of three periods of class time interruption is allow-
able per student.
   9.   The Rudolph Instrument is available only to credentialed
counselors or registered psychologists.

   B. Begin with top level function 1.0 (see Fig. 5.11) and ask, "What
steps must be taken (by someone or something) to accomplish 1.0?" Just
as the functions to be performed in the mission profile were identified,
start by identifying the product or outcome for *that* function (i.e., 1.0)
and then identify all functions required to achieve the function[4] (see Fig.
5.12).
   In preparing the function flow block diagrams, we use the concept of
the discrepancy analysis once more. Each function identified in the mission
profile represents a subproduct to be achieved. In function analysis we
determine exactly the subfunction (or sub-subproducts) required to accomplish that subfunction, and we have as this referent a discrepancy
analysis of the difference between where we are now and what has to be
done to eliminate that discrepancy. The process is like doing a "mini-
mission analysis" at each level of the function analysis procedure. Each
function has its own objective and its own performance requirements, and
we can draw a mini-mission profile for accomplishing each function.
   The processes utilized in the various levels of system analysis differ
only in degree, not in kind—we repeat the same process over and over as
we identify and define all the requirements for meeting the set need and
selected problem. The elements, again, are:

   1.   Identify what is required for each function or subfunction.
   2.   Identify the status quo for each function and subfunction.
   3.   Identify functions or subfunctions necessary to meet the requirements for completion of that function (or subfunction) *and*
additional performance requirements for the achievement of *that*
function.

   *4. The analyst at this point and throughout the analysis phase is assuming
a role similar to that of composer. He is in one segment of the planning phase
and should not confuse that role with the doing phase. To successfully play the
role of planner, assume that on completion of the planning phase you are leaving
the area and that your plans will be carried out by others without your assistance;
then you will not be apt to confuse the identification of what must be done with
the actual doing of it.*

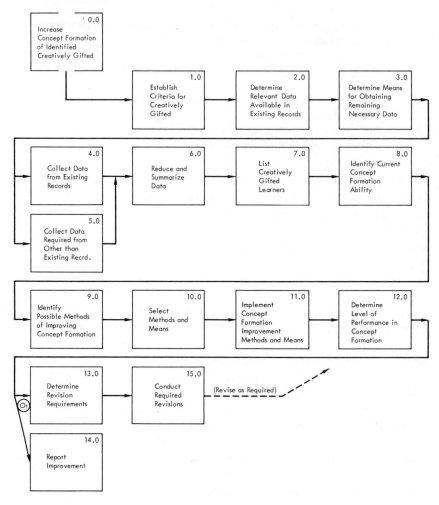

FIG. 5.11. A possible mission profile for identifying creatively gifted learners and improving concept formation.

4. List the functions (or subfunctions) in their proper chronology so that order, sequence, and interrelations may be determined visually (this uses the tools and formating of function flow block diagramming).

C. Proceed with function 2.0, then 3.0, and so on, until the top level of analysis (mission profile) has been completed and any additional performance requirements have been listed by function number.

D. Check all the previous functions that have been "broken out" with the mission objective and performance requirements. This process represents a check for internal consistency, a broad inquiry whether it is

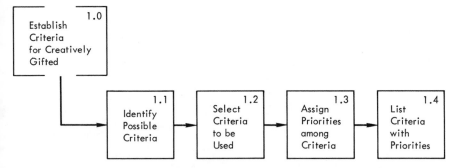

FIG. 5.12.   Function analysis: note that the box for 1.0 is open, indicating that it is a reference function.

still feasible to continue, and an examination of the analysis to determine if more performance requirements exist. When the product is *temporarily* satisfactory, proceed to the first level of analysis.

E. In the same manner as in step B (p. 89) attend to the break-out of functions necessary to accomplish function 1.1, then 1.2, etc. Fig. 5.13 shows the first-level analysis of function 1.2 into its lower-level functions. The following format is suggested for listing additional performance requirements uncovered during function analysis:

Function and Number	*Performance Requirements*
1.2.1 Obtain established criteria from existing studies.	*a.* Existing studies from district library and county library will be used exclusively.
1.2.2. Obtain criteria from other sources.	*a.* "Other" sources will be approved by Assistant Superintendent for Instruction.
	b. Project must be completed by February.
1.2.3. List all criteria.	*a.* Same as 1.2.1 and 1.2.2.

F. When the first level has been completed, check for internal consistency as in the top level.

G. Continue downward to the succeeding lower levels of analysis until the functions are finite enough to take on the appearance of individual units rather than sets or groups of actions. When this level of analysis has been reached, stop. It is now time to begin the task analysis (see Chapter 6). Check back and forth, upward and downward, continually asking, "can it realistically happen this way" and still meet the mission objective and its performance requirements? It must also be determined whether all the components (functions) *interact* properly. Does the mission

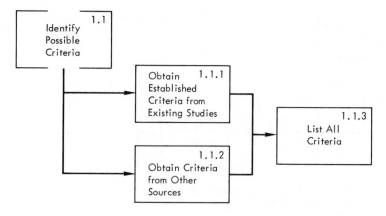

FIG. 5.13.

and the analysis still make sense? Can it work? Fig. 5.14 displays the circular checking process.

H. Draw a summary flow diagram of functions at various levels, in the order in which the functions are performed, and showing critical feedback and interaction pathways. (Be prepared to revise it.) List all additional performance requirements separately by function number. Often, in a large analysis, parts of the analysis at lower levels are performed separately and brought together. The success of the resulting mesh (or interface) depends, in part, on adequate review of the final flow diagram to make sure that all subsystems interact properly. Always be critical—question and require justification for everything. The flow charts at the end of this chapter (Figs. 5.17 and 5.18) show the function "break-outs" for several selected examples. The mission profiles for these examples were presented in Chapter 4. These charts represent partial function analysis for some of the functions shown in the plans for the Mexican–American Project and the individualization of learning project mission profiles.

The function analysis shown in Fig. 5.17 derives from the mission profile presented in Chapter 4. It is but a partial analysis to show the method of function analysis and only some of the "break-outs" appear (functions 3.0, 4.0, 17.0 and 18.0 are thus only depicted here). In addition,

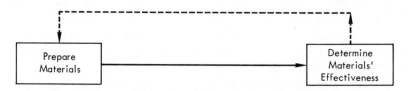

FIG. 5.14.   Note feedback requirements—is it possible that the results of a later block will require a change in an earlier block?

Fig. 5.17 shows lower-level function analysis for 18.0 to further indicate the fact that function analysis may go to several levels; for instance, function 18.0 is broken down to the fourth level (cf. 18.1.1.2.1) as an example of this continuing analysis process. It should also be noted that in function analysis, as in all of the other system analysis phases, only "what" is to be done is indicated, not "how" to get it accomplished.

The function analysis shown in Fig. 5.18 is derived from the mission profile shown also in Chapter 4. In this case, as an example of function analysis, function number 12.0 is broken down into the first level of analysis, and functions 12.2 and 12.3 are broken down to the second level of analysis.

There is often the misconception that the "top level" analysis is mission analysis, the next level of analysis is function analysis, and the next lower level is task analysis; this is not so! Function analysis continues until the resulting functions are no longer clusters of outcomes but are single units of performance. These single units of performance are arbitrarily called "tasks." Therefore, function analysis usually has several levels of break-outs until task analysis is reached. Task analysis is covered in some detail in Chapter 6.

Summary and Review

Function analysis is the process of breaking each function into its component parts while identifying interactions. Function analysis really commences during the mission analysis when the mission profile is derived. The mission profile is also known as the top level of function analysis.

Function analysis formally proceeds from the analysis of the functions identified in the mission profile. These functions come from the mission profile and may be called subfunctions, since they do derive from higher-level (or top) functions.

Function analysis continues until all the functions have been analyzed and identified for all the top-level (mission profile) functions. This tells *what* must be done to achieve each top-level function. All the functions, subfunctions, and so on are revealed until vertical expansion of the mission profile is complete. Then all the functions describing *what* has to be done to meet the mission objective and its performance requirements are identified.

Each time a function from the function analysis is identified, the performance requirements for it must be specified. That is, one must identify in precise, measurable terms what must be done to accomplish a given function. This performance requirement identification for each function

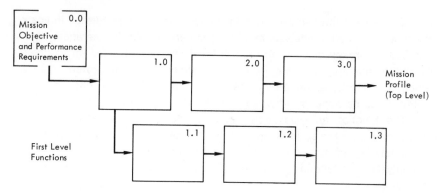

FIG. 5.15.

resembles that which is accomplished in identifying the performance requirements for the mission except that it occurs at each lower-level function that is analyzed and named. There is a continuous process of determining *what* must be done, as well as the criteria for accomplishment and the kinds of lower-order "things" that constitute the function. This continuous, layer-by-layer determination may be shown diagrammatically (see Fig. 5.15). Each function, from the first level through the task analysis level (see Chapter 6) requires the identification and listing of performance requirements. One way to perceive function analysis is that, at each lower level, one is determining a mission profile for that function and deriving performance requirements for that "miniature mission." Viewed in this manner, each function shows a "mission" of its own, and each must have a precise definition of the performance requirements for its successful completion. As the analysis moves down, each function or subfunction becomes identified as a product or subproduct, including performance requirements for each function or subfunction.

The differences between analyses at the various levels is a matter of degree rather than kind; there really is no difference between a mission profile and the function analysis of any one of its functions. That is, the process is exactly the same, only the actual functions differ. Miniature or subordinant "missions" are identified each time a function is "broken out." Performance requirements must be set for each function even if it is the very first one—performance requirements of the mission—or the very last function that can be broken out before deriving tasks.

In function analysis, as in mission analysis, the job is to identify the major milestones for achieving a function and to identify the criteria (the performance requirements) by which one knows when a function has been successfully performed or completed.

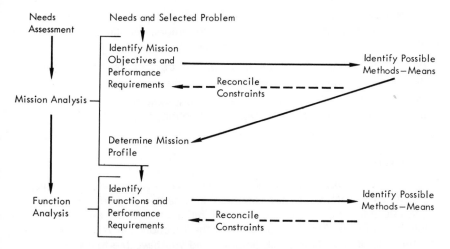

FIG. 5.16. A diagrammatic representation of the relationship between mission analysis, function analysis, and methods-means analysis. Based on Kaufman (1968).

Function Analysis and Feasibility

A Preview of Methods–Means Analysis

Each time a function (or a family of functions) and its performance requirements are identified, it becomes necessary to check the methods–means "data bank" and determine whether a possible methods–means exists for achieving those requirements. (This subject is further detailed in Chapter 7 on methods–means analysis.)

If there is one or more possible methods–means, then we may continue the function analysis to the next level. However, if there is not at least one possible methods–means, we have a constraint that must be reconciled before proceeding to the next level.

There is a requirement for constant checking back through previous steps and data and to the original needs statement to assure that the final identification of "whats" will be internally consistent and have external validity. That is, it must be determined that all the functions are compatible with one another as well as with the need, the problem, and other functions at all levels. Fig. 5.16 summarizes both mission analysis and function analysis.

Glossary

Function: one of a group of related outcomes (or products or subproducts) contributing to a larger outcome (or product).

Function flow block diagram: the diagrammatic representation of functions that show the order and relations among functions. The order is shown by the numbers and the solid lines.

Parallel functions: functions that can go on simultaneously or in the absence of a required order of accomplishment.

Series functions: functions related to one another in linear and dependent fashion. An example might be Christmas tree lights.

Exercises

1. Given a mission objective, performance requirements, and mission profile as developed in the exercise in Chapter 4, perform a function analysis adhering to the five rules of function analysis and maintaining functional levels. The final product of the function analysis will be in the form of a function flow block diagram and will have the following characteristics:

1. All functions derived are in a logical sequence.

2. All blocks are square or rectangular.

3. All blocks contain an appropriate number.

4. All blocks are connected with solid lines.

5. All feedback functions are designated by broken lines.

6. All functions in series sequence are shown in horizontal sequence.

7. All parallel sequences are shown in vertical sequence.

8. All numbers are by function level and identified according to the "parent" higher-level function, following a decimal pattern.

9. All alternate functions are designated by an "OR" gate enclosed in a circle.

10. No function is broken out into only one subfunction.

11. Each function derived contains at least one verb.

12. All subfunctions derived provide for the accomplishment of the "parent" higher-level function.

13. All interactions or reference functions are shown as "open" boxes.

2. For each item on the left, place the letter corresponding to the item's use in *connecting* functions in flow block diagramming (as named on the right) in the appropriate blank.

_____ vertical lines   *a.* interaction or reference function

_____ broken lines   *b.* alternate sequence

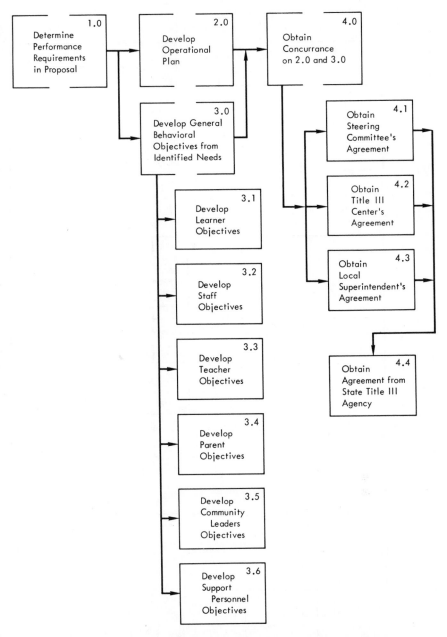

FIG. 5.17. An example of a function analysis for a Mexican-American education project showing the "break-outs" of functions from the top or mission profile level of analysis. Note the differences between parallel functions, which may go on simultaneously, and series functions, which must proceed in a specified order of accomplishment. After Wasco Union School District project.

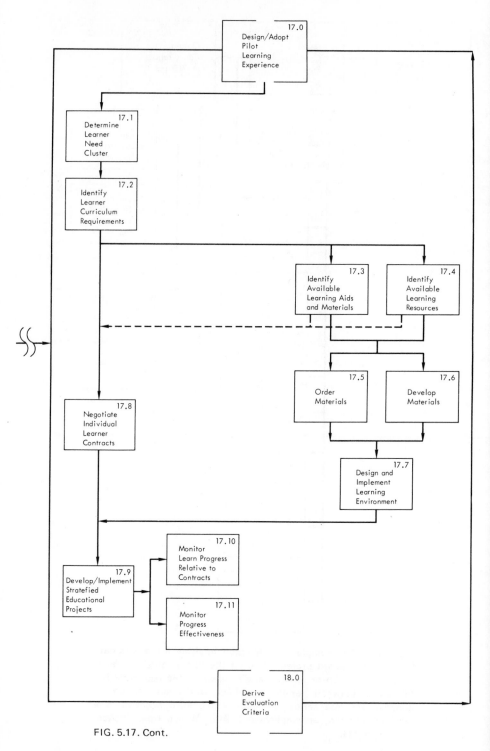

FIG. 5.17. Cont.

98

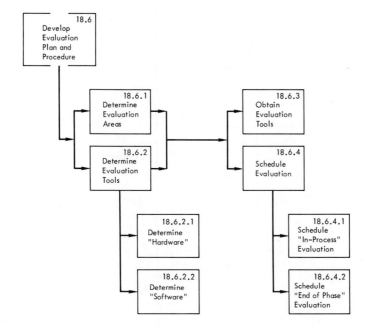

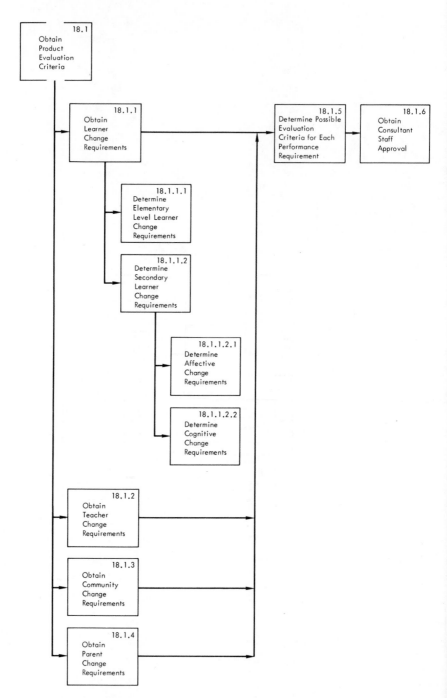

FIG. 5.17. Cont.

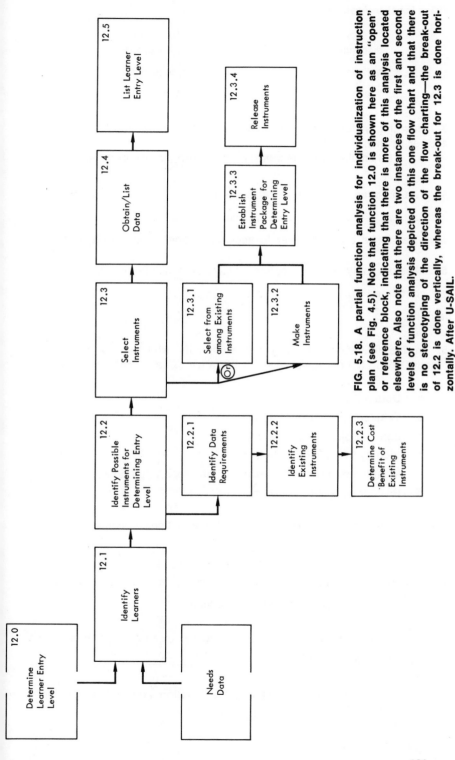

FIG. 5.18. A partial function analysis for individualization of instruction plan (see Fig. 4.5). Note that function 12.0 is shown here as an "open" or reference block, indicating that there is more of this analysis located elsewhere. Also note that there are two instances of the first and second levels of function analysis depicted on this one flow chart and that there is no stereotyping of the direction of the flow charting—the break-out of 12.2 is done vertically, whereas the break-out for 12.3 is done horizontally. After U-SAIL.

_____ diagonal lines   c. parallel functions

_____ horizontal lines   d. series sequence

_____ "open" box   e. feedback loop (path)

3. How many function(s) must all functions break into? (*Select best answer below*).
(a) smaller; (b) one more; (c) two more; (d) two or more.

4. The purpose of function analysis is to _____,

_____, and _____

what has to be done in order to accomplish the mission objective.

5. Mission analysis and function analysis are similar in that they both are concerned about _____ be done.

6. In the following functions below, specify whether the function is "higher level" (H) or "lower level" (L) relative to each other in this group:

a. Obtain Ph.D.
b. Take comprehensive exams.
c. Select topic for term paper.
d. Identify instruction criteria.
e. Identify comprehensive examination preparation courses.
f. Pass comprehensive exams.

7. In a function flow block diagram, a broken line indicates _____

_____.

8. In performing a function analysis, the analyst attends to _____ _____ levels of analysis at a time.

9. In referencing to a higher-order function or to another function at the same level, the box is left _____.

10. The numbering system used in the function analysis is done in a _____ fashion.

Answer Briefly the Following Questions:

11. What is the role of the function analysis?

12. How does the function analysis relate to the mission analysis?

13. What part does "check—recheck—revise" play in a function analysis?

14. When an analyst has completed a function analysis, what does he have?

15. State the five rules for making a function flow block diagram.

True and False

16. Functions found in the mission profile are called first-level functions.

_____

17. Breaking-out a function identifies subordinate "mini"-missions.

_____

18. Each function has performance requirements. _____

19. Interactions are not shown on a function flow block diagram.

_____

20. Each function must be identifiable as discrete. _____

Fill in the Blanks

21. To communicate with others, each block must contain at least one

_____ term.

22. Mission objective is identified in a function flow block diagram as the number _____.

23. Open blocks are also known as _____ blocks.

24. Each block must be _____ in shape.

25. Give an example of the numbering system used in function flow block diagrams: _____.

26. In one sentence, define a function: _____

_____

27. In one sentence, define the function of an "OR" gate. _____

_____

28. Open blocks indicate which of the following functions?

    a. Input

    b. Feedback

    c. Output

    d. Parallel functions

29. When working on function analysis, the system analyst attempts:

    a. To break one function out all the way down to the task level.

    b. To focus on one level of function analysis until those of equal magnitude have been identified.

    c. To identify all tasks to be done.

Fill in the Blanks

30. In performing a function analysis, the analyst is identifying the _____ and not the _____.

31. The top level of a function analysis is called the _____

_____.

32. In order to begin a function analysis, the analyst requires the following three things:

    a. _____

    b. _____

    c. _____

33. The process of checking for internal consistency is called _____

_____.

34. If two or more functions are or can be performed simultaneously, they are said to be in _____ sequence.

35. Functions that must be performed one after the other are said to be in _____ sequence.

36. Take one of the mission profiles presented in Chapter 4, perform a function analysis on it, and produce a function flow block diagram. Take the analysis down through at least the second level of analysis.

For one second-level function, continue the function analysis down through the task analysis level. (This is called a "single-thread analysis.") Each function identified must have performance requirements—use the additional performance requirements form on page 58.

task analysis

chapter 6

Tasks may be defined as units of performance which, when collected, constitute a function. Thus task listing and description (here collectively called task analysis) form the final "breaking-down" step in system analysis, and it emanates from the lowest level of function identified before "units of performance" are identified.

As indicated earlier, the difference between mission analysis, function analysis, and task analysis is a difference of degree rather than of kind. Using the previous analogy of a microscope, we recall that each time a function is examined under a greater degree of magnification, more detail is visible; a task, then, is the lowest level of detail in a system analysis. It is the lowest level of analysis that will indicate *what* must be done to get a higher-order function accomplished. (Another analogy may be considered; a bead is to a necklace as a task is to a function.)

The tasks are derived from the total on-going system analysis process, where (1) an overall product or outcome was identified in the mission objective and its performance requirements, (2) the basic functions required to accomplish the mission were identified (the mission profile), and (3) each of these basic (or top-level) functions was analyzed to determine the requisite lower-order subfunctions. Finally, each identified function and subfunction may be broken down into single facets, or units of performance, and these may be listed and analyzed to determine the final, lowest level of performance requirements to accomplish each. The relation of task analysis to mission analysis and function analysis is shown in Fig. 6.1.

When the detailed analysis is at the task level and all the performance requirements are identified for each of the tasks, the educational planner has, for the first time, determined all the "whats" for successful problem solution. Task analysis then provides the complete array of "what is to be

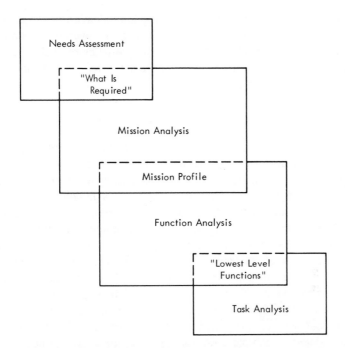

FIG. 6.1.   The basic steps of analysis showing the "linkages" (bordered by a broken line) or joining aspects, which relate the levels.

done" down to the level of understanding actual requirements for implementation of the plan.

The Two Basic Steps of Task Analysis

Task analysis may be conceived of as occurring in two basic steps:

1.   Identifying the basic tasks (or steps) involved in accomplishing an overall function.
2.   Determining the characteristics of the tasks, their requirements, and their context, and putting these in a time-ordered sequence.

Some authors [for instance, Mager and Beach (1967)] use the nomenclature of "task listing" and "task detailing." The task steps are listed, and then such things as type of performance and learning difficulty are determined as part of the task-detailing process. Any useful task analysis should include a comparable two-step process. Here the two steps are called task listing and task description.

Task listing, of course, consists of the identification of the basic sub-elements or steps involved in accomplishing an overall function. *Task description* is the determination of the characteristics of each of the tasks or steps, including the context and requirements for accomplishment and the time relationships and criticality of each.

Task Listing

The listing of the tasks (or units of performance) that constitute a given function can be thought of as a check list, a sequential listing of tasks that, taken together, will yield the overall function from which they derive. An example of a task listing might be a hypothetical check list for test construction using item analysis as a part of the test construction process. Rederiving this hypothetical example, one might conceive of an overall mission that would require construction of a test—say the mission was one of determining criteria for predicting successful performance in graduate school, to be used in an ordinary classroom situation. There would be, then, a mission objective, performance requirement, a mission profile, function analysis (including additional associated performance requirements), and finally a lower level function indicating the requirement to complete an item analysis for a hypothetical test. The hypothetical "check list" or task listing might be something like the following:

1. List the test item numbers.

2. Mark another column as test alternatives *a, b, c,* and *d.*

3. Enter on the summary sheet, for each test and for each item, the incorrect alternatives selected for each item.

4. Sum up the incorrect alternatives selected for each item and for each possible alternative (*a, b, c,* and *d*).

5. Identify the ten most frequently missed test items by summing across alternatives missed for each test item.

6. Identify the frequency of the missed alternatives selected for each test item in the "top ten."

7. Prepare a summary listing of the data collected for the item analysis for this test.

It should be noted that the listing avoids determining *how* the tasks are to be performed, nor did it indicate that any could or should be done by a computer, although the possibility exists. The purpose of the task listing is merely to identify the tasks to be accomplished, regardless of who or what is to become involved. In actuality, tasks could be accomplished by people, equipment, or people and equipment. It is *not* the purpose of a task analysis or a task listing to identify *how* a task will be performed, but only to name the tasks and the order they are to be performed.

In this initial listing (or check-list phase) other data may be collected. For instance, Mager and Beach (1967) suggest the determination of "frequency of performance," "importance," and "learning difficulty" for each of the tasks identified. This procedure would seem to be especially useful when one is designing curriculum, or a training program per se. However, for most educational planning requirements, the simple listing of task components provides sufficient information for most task analyses.

If it is decided that the definition of "what is to be done" is complete enough after the accomplishment of task listing, then, as with other steps of system analysis, the analyst should list on a separate sheet the performance requirements associated with each task. The task analysis is completed when the performance requirements have been determined.

Task Description[1]

After the task listing has been obtained, the next step is (or could be) to determine the salient characteristics of the tasks involved. For instance, there might be such important considerations as the environment in which a task or series of tasks is to be performed, physical requirements, health and safety requirements, nature of the stimulus that signals that the task should begin, the nature and type of response that is required, the time requirements for the beginning and ending of a task, and the order and relationship between the tasks and/or subtasks.

For this reason, the task description generally takes the information from the task listing, arranges it on a time-based scale, and identifies the outstanding characteristics of the task and the context in which it is to be accomplished. As an example for a generic task analysis, the following items might require detailed specification in the task description phase, and the completion of the task analysis would oblige the system analyst (or planner) to provide these data (or more). Such a tentative list to consider in the task description phase would be:

1. Stimulus characteristics that "signal" the requirement to begin or start.

2. Response characteristics of the required output, including whether it requires a binary (yes-no or on-off) response, a simple manipulation, a discrimination, a complex hand–eye or psychomotor coordination, or no response at all.

---

1. *Task description may be especially useful in system synthesis, after the methods–means have been selected and further definition of the selected methods–means (for instance, a programmed instructional sequence) is required.*

3. Force or energy requirements.

4. Physiological, medical, or health consideration (if people might be involved).

5. Location for task, such as indoors, outdoors, in snow, at designed workspace, or in any number of a variety of locations.

6. Tools, devices, or instruments that are necessarily involved in the performace of the task.

7. Other data inputs required for the successful completion of the task.

8. Time requirements.

9. Criticality of the task—would the total mission be destroyed if this task were not accomplished correctly the first time, or could it be redone if performed incorrectly or out of sequence.

By and large, task description charts are prepared for this phase of task analysis. Many and varied task analysis formats may be used, and selection depends on the required results of the analysis. Such formats vary from a basic and simple one suggested by Mager and Beach (1967), which utilizes four columns—(1) task number, (2) steps in performing the task, (3) type of performance, and (4) learning difficulty—to quite complex man–machine interaction formats used in the aerospace field, which might include detailed physiological and psychological considerations and relationships.

The format selected by the planner should be only as complex as is necessary to supply the data required in the planning process itself. The important thing to remember and include in the task description is that it *must* specify the total requirements for accomplishing the task. Remember that the purpose of performing a system analysis is to identify the requirements for the accomplishment of a given mission. The system analysis process indicates all the parts and the relations between the parts of accomplishing a given mission. Thus system analysis reveals, in layers, the subsystems or portions involved in mission accomplishment and the requirements for performing each. If a task analysis does not include the performance requirements for each task or task element, then it is nothing more than a gross descriptor and does not provide the detailed information and criteria that would further assure that the analysis product will be functional for determining the most relevant and practical possibilities (methods and means) for accomplishing the mission. The task analysis is of considerable usefulness in system synthesis, especially having a direct input into network-based techniques for management and control (see Chapter 8 for further detail concerning the relation between such tools as PERT and a system approach). Table 6.1 presents a hypothetical task description for an administrative function. It represents an *arbitrary* selection of a task-analysis format. The steps for performing such a task description are as follows:

Step 1:   List all the tasks and subtasks necessary to accomplish the function being analyzed. This is the same derivation process employed in the break-out of the mission profile and the function analysis. The tasks identified are placed in sequence, *the order in which they will occur.* In identifying the tasks, we want to make them independent, so there will be no (or minimal) overlap. This is the *task-listing* process.

Step 2:   List, *by tasks*, the stimulus requirements (if relevant). These are the "input" requirements, the data required by the "operator" (or "doer" of the task when it is assigned) to perform the tasks. State what form the data will or must be in to be usable.

Step 3:   List the response requirements (the action requirements). These are the operations, the number of times each will occur, and the time necessary to perform the operation, if time is a real consideration.

Step 4:   By task, list the support requirements. These are the *kinds* of materials and equipment necessary to support the operation of the task and the *types* of personnel or equipment required as "operators."

Step 5:   List the performance criteria. Here is the specification of the product (or outcome) of the task. Just as a mission will produce a product, and a function will produce a product (or subproduct), so will a task produce a product—a performance outcome. The performance requirements of the product of the task may be such items as (1) no errors, (2) list must contain all items, (3) copy must be nonsmudged and readable, and (4) form must have adequate space for teacher notations.

Step 6:   Specify the prerequisite knowledges and/or skills the operator must have in order to be able to perform a given task. If, for example, in the preparation of proposal there is a necessity for a high skill level of art work, then advanced art capability may be a critical requirement and as such is a prerequisite that must be noted.

As a matter of practice, the lowest-level subfunction that is being analyzed at the task level is always identified by the function number. This function number (e.g. 4.1.1.) is usually placed in the upper left-hand corner of the form. Failure to identify the function being analyzed will have obvious consequences.

TABLE 6.1. Example of an Administrative Task Analysis

Administrative Tasks

Subfunction 4.1.1

Task (in performance or "doing" terms)	Input (Stimulus) Requirements		Response (Action) Requirements		Time	Materials	Support Requirements		Performance Criteria	Prerequisite Knowledge or Skill Requirement
	Data	Form	Operation	No.			Equipment	Personnel		
Obtain list of items	Items from 2.0		Physically pick up	1				Clerk	None	None
Sequence Items	Items on last cumulative folder sequence		Note relevant cumulative sequence			Paper, pencil		Clerk	Include all items, sequence follows cumulative sequence	None
			List items in order	1						
Design format	Sequence of items		Locate name column	1		Paper, pencil, ruler		Draftsman	Space for all items	Elementary drafting skill
			Count items	1						
			Measure paper						Adequate notation space in each column	
			Divide space available by items	1						
			Locate items columns							
Prepare Reproducible	Data form with items		Select	1		Stencil correction fluid, ruler, stylus	Type-writer	Typist	No errors	Knowledge of stencil preparation
			Reproducible, adjust, and align	1						
			Prepare	1						
			Rule columns							
Reproduce data form	Reproducible		Obtain paper	1		Paper	Offset press	Pressman	Readable, non-smudged copy	Skill in operation of offset press
Store on shelf			Run press	1						

Summary

Task analysis is the "lowest level" of a system analysis; it derives from a mission analysis and the related function analysis and thus provides the final level of detail required to identify all the "whats" for problem solution.

Task analysis consists of two subparts, that relating to the identification and ordering of the steps to be taken (task listing) and that which identifies the salient characteristics and requirements of successful task accomplishment (task description). Together, these two parts constitute a task analysis that tells what units of performance are to be accomplished and the performance requirements associated with each task. Frequently, the task listing along with its performance requirements will suffice for the task analysis.

The format for conducting and reporting a task analysis is not firm or fixed. The format should be designed (or selected) to ensure that the relevant data for planning decision making are provided to the system planner. It is critical that any format utilized provide data on the nature of the task and the performance requirements (specifications) for the successful completion of each task.

The difference between mission analysis, function analysis, and task analysis is a difference in degree rather than in kind. The task analysis is basically accomplished in the same manner as is the mission analysis and the function analysis—it is an identification and breaking down of the elements required to accomplish something. In task analysis, however, more detailed performance information is obtained and reported; for this will provide, by and large, the basic structure and information for the actual design, implementation, test, and evaluation of the educational plan when put into operation.

Task Analysis, Function Analysis, Mission Analysis, and Their Relationship

The three system analysis tools we have considered so far are all concerned with determining "what" is to be accomplished to get us, effectively and efficiently, from where we are to meeting the identified and selected needs. The analysis proceeds in layers, or levels, to determine all the requirements for successful problem solution by identifying all the aspects of the problem and setting detailed specifications for the resolution of the problem.

Performance requirements: As with the preceding steps of mission analysis and function analysis, task analysis requires the determination of

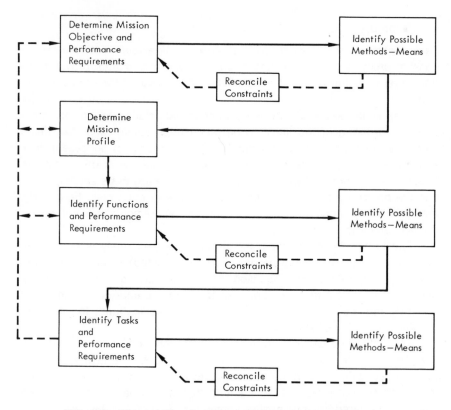

FIG. 6.2. The relation between mission, function, task, and methods–means analysis. When accomplished in "parallel" with the methods–means analysis, the system analysis process provides an on-going feasibility determination. After R. Kaufman (1970a).

measurable specifications—performance requirements. In the task analysis process, however, the determination of these specifications is formalized in the task analysis format that is actually selected. Task analysis and methods–means analysis—each system analysis step, as we see in detail in the chapter on methods–means analysis, may perform an on-going feasibility study by determining, at each stage of analysis, if there are any methods and means (strategies and tools) to accomplish the functions (or tasks) and their associated performance requirements. Task analysis is no exception.

Because task analysis is the final "breaking-down" step in system analysis, the final feasibility analysis is completed after tasks and their specifications have been delineated. Fig. 6.2 is the final diagram relating mission, function, task, and methods–means analysis.

Mission, function, and task analyses; deciding on levels: The difference between mission, function, and task analysis is arbitrary and depends on each starting place. One possible way of knowing when you have reached the task level is to ask yourself "if I break it down any further, would I have to start stating 'how' the job would have to be done." If the answer would be "yes," stop, you are at the task level. An analysis should only be carried down to the level necessary for the analyst to be reasonably assured that he will "get back" the necessary information required for decision making.

Exercises

1. Given a function analysis derived in Chapter 5, perform a task analysis. The task analysis form will be generated by the analyst and will be related to the particular function(s) being analyzed. The task analysis will have the following characteristics:

1. All tasks identified will be listed in sequential order.

2. All performance requirements of each task will be listed.

3. Any necessary stimulus to perform the task will be listed.

4. Support requirements will be listed.

5. Prerequisite knowledges and skills will be listed, if appropriate to the performance of the task.

2. A task analysis begins with the completion of the _____

_____.

3. A task analysis derives units of _____ called tasks.

4. A task analysis may be considered as having two components. These are, in order (1) _____ and (2) _____

_____.

5. After listing the tasks, the analyst identifies the characteristics of the product of the tasks, or the _____

_____.

6. Each task analysis will differ according to the requirements of the _____ being analyzed.

7. How does task analysis relate to the previous areas developed—mission analysis, mission profile, and function analysis?

8. Assuming that you are to do a task analysis of a series of functions generated by a function analysis, outline all the headings on the form you would devise for your task assignment.

9. What determines the areas of consideration in a task analysis?

10. State in some detail the specific differences between a function analysis and a task analysis.

11. Select any two functions, at the lowest level, from the function analysis you have completed. Develop a task analysis form that will be responsive to the requirements of those particular functions and then perform a task analysis on each of the functions selected.

methods-means
analysis

chapter 7

Mission analysis, function analysis, and task analysis are process tools with which a planner identifies and documents those functions and tasks which must be performed in order to ensure the predictable accomplishment of a mission objective. These processes attend to the identification of the "whats"; but when "whats" are derived, it is necessary to ascertain whether there exists, or could exist, one or more strategies and/or vehicles by which they may be accomplished. The system planner not only wants to identify what has to be done and in what order, he also wants ultimately to be able to select the "best possible" way.

In order to provide the educational system designer with the information necessary to make the most intelligent selection of ways to complete each function, a listing of alternate strategies and vehicles (methods and means), with the advantages and disadvantages of each, is compiled. This compilation serves as a data bank from which the system designer will be able to later make his selection. The process by which the data bank is produced is called *methods–means analysis.*

A "method" is the strategy for achieving some performance requirements, and a "means" is the vehicle by which a strategy is achieved. If we were considering a curriculum problem in, say reading, then information from a system analysis would provide performance requirements for terminal or final success. From these performance requirements, it would be possible to identify (1) requirements for mastery of content, (2) demonstrable skills and knowledges, (3) characteristics of the population for which the behavior change program is to be designed, and (4) the required nature of the context and environment in which the program is to be conducted. In short, we would have a data base for determining the maximum possible number of the strategies (methods) and vehicles (means) for achieving the performance requirements. A *possible* "method" for achieving these hypothetical performance requirements in reading would be "individualized instruction," which would be responsive to each individual learner's backgrounds and entry skills. A *possible* "vehicle" for implementing this strategy (method) might be programmed self-instructional materials, using a responsive device to enable the program to "branch" to remedial and additional materials, as the students' responses dictated relative to the predetermined performance requirements. Another possible methods–means combination might be a tutor in a reading laboratory utilizing tachistoscopes, tapes, and special reading materials. Still other methods–means combinations might meet the performance requirements. Thus a methods–means analysis identifies the possible strategies and vehicles for meeting performance requirements and lists the advantages and disadvantages of each.

What Is a Methods–Means Analysis?

A methods–means analysis is the identification of the maximum possible number of methods and the advantages and disadvantages of each for achieving the specified performance requirement(s) identified in a system analysis. It is best in a system analysis if at least a cursory methods–means analysis occurs continually at each phase of the analysis in order to assure that there are no constraints arising from the inability to identify and select a feasible methods–means for achieving the identified performance requirements.

The methods–means analysis *does not* select *how* the requirement will be met, it only names the possible methods–means for achieving the performance requirements. The "how" selection is made during *system synthesis* and is not here considered part of planning via system analysis.

When Is the Methods–Means Analysis Begun?

In performing a system analysis, the methods–means analysis *best begins* as soon as performance requirements for a product (or outcome) have been identified—ordinarily, immediately after the setting of one or more of the performance requirements for the overall mission. Once the final outcome (product) has been identified, the next action is to find out if there are any possible strategies and vehicles for accomplishing the requirements. This may be viewed as an identification of the requirements for "product" which, in turn, is matched against the requirements for "process" to achieve the product. The methods–means may already exist, or it might be something that is in development and will be ready at a future time or something that has to be "invented" and is "inventable."

If a performance requirement is achievable, further analysis continues. *If not, then there exists a constraint that must be reconciled before we continue.* This operational removal (or reconciliation) of a constraint may be accomplished only by (1) changing the performance requirement, (2) finding a possible methods–means to achieve the performance requirement, (3) redefining the limits within which the performance requirements may be met, or if none of these is possible, (4) stopping the activity then and there.

A methods–means analysis may begin whenever the analyst chooses. The experienced educational planner will undoubtedly find greater utility in starting the methods–means analysis as soon as a mission objective and associated performance requirements have been identified and stated. Thus, continual identification of *possible* "hows" and the relative advantages and disadvantages of each, means that an ongoing *feasibility assessment* is being conducted (see Fig. 7.1). As the system analysis continues, and as the methods–means analysis portion coincides, there is continuous checking and assurance that it is feasible to suppose that mission can be accomplished.

When the planner has completed the task analysis and the final methods–means analysis, there are two products:

1.   A data base of *feasible "whats"* for problem solution.

2.   A data base of *possible "hows"* and the advantages and disadvantages of each.

A diagrammatic representation of the relation between a mission, function, and task analysis and methods–means analysis appears in Fig. 7.1, which indicates that the methods–means analysis is "parallel" to the determination of the mission, the functions, and the tasks on an ongoing basis. Fig. 7.2 is a process diagram of the relations between any analytical step in a system analysis and the conduct of a methods–means analysis.

An Option

In conducting a system analysis in educational planning, at the option of the planner, the methods–means analysis may be conducted *after* all the functions and tasks have been identified and the performance requirements for each have been determined and listed. Accepting this option may have several advantages. First, there is little (or perhaps less) distraction from the identification of "what is to be done" and no risk of the possible distraction of selecting or even identifying how each performance requirement is to be accomplished. This is to say that often a planning team, "forgetting" that the methods–means analysis does *not* select the methods–means for achieving the performance requirements,

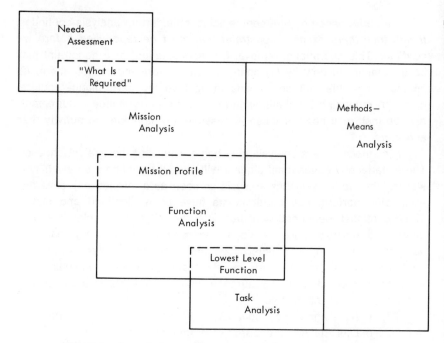

FIG. 7.1. As mission, function, and task analyses continue, there may be a parallel methods–means analysis. Each time a performance requirement (or family of performance requirements) is identified, possible methods–means may also be identified.

"cheats" the process by prematurely selecting the "how." To avoid this risk, or to avoid the problem of possibly mixing "whats" and "hows," the methods–means analysis may be delayed until all functions, tasks, and performance requirements have been identified.

Another possible reason for delaying the methods–means analysis is for purposes of teaching new planner/analysts the skills of system analysis. Newcomers to system analysis almost always want to "jump into" the selection of methods and means before requirements have been identified. Frequently it is easier to keep a new system analyst's attention on identifying "what" by doing the mission, function, and task analyses first, and identifying the possible "hows" last.

In reality, the tendency to determine feasibility by conducting a methods–means analysis after the identification of each performance requirement or a related group of performance requirements (a family of performance requirements) is generally best. The continuous attesting to feasibility may save considerable time and labor, especially if a non-reconcilable constraint is identified and system planning is drastically changed or stopped.

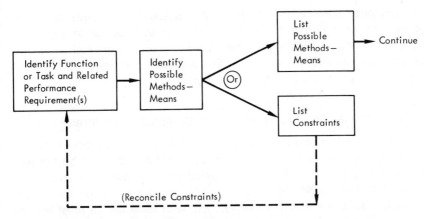

FIG. 7.2. A process for performing methods–means analysis during system analysis.

From What Source Does Methods–Means Information Come?

Methods–means information is found wherever valid data may be obtained. A number of texts, especially those from audio-visual education, discuss "means" at great length and in great detail, primarily for instructional problems. Concerning other methods–means, one might well consult specialists, vendors, literature in education, and literature in other fields. This area of identification of appropriate tools and strategies is the chance to "brainstorm." Here we are not fettered by "the way it's always been done," and we may explore ideas that might superficially seem extreme to determine if a vehicle and/or a strategy *might* be usable and possibly practical to meet the performance requirements. List all the possible methods–means for each requirement.

Must a Methods–Means Analysis Be Done for Each Function and Each Task?

Ideally, each performance requirement should be matched with possible methods–means. In fact, each and every requirement *must* be met. Often, performance requirements are related in "families"—they are related and may be lumped together for identifying appropriate methods and means. Although each performance requirement must be met, the frequency of accomplishing the methods–means analysis depends on the analyst. Final methods–means possibilities can only be determined at the *task analysis* level, and all preceding identifications of methods–means consist of progressively precise determination.

The methods–means analysis may be done for each function, for a group of functions, or even for an analysis level. However, remember that the methods–means analysis will identify possible constraints that may jeopardize the accomplishment of the mission in whole or in part. This constant check on feasibility is central and critical to the validity of the system analysis and, therefore, to the successful completion of the mission. Don't try to fool yourself or the analysis!

How Are the Methods–Means Data Compiled and Stored?

In a function flow block diagram, each function is associated with a function block. Thus 0.0 would be for the mission, 1.0 would be the first function in the mission profile, 1.2 would be a derivative function from block 1.0, and so on. For each function, the analyst must record the function flow block diagram number, and with each list he must list the performance requirements for the particular function on a methods–means form (see Table 7.1). He should designate these performance requirements by letter (1.1-A, 1.1-B, or 3.1-A). For each alphanumerically identified performance requirement, it is necessary to list next to it the methods and means that *could* be used to meet the requirement. These data will build up for each functional unit as the analysis continues. This record-keeping will ultimately result in a compendium of possible methods and means combinations for each performance requirement (or performance requirement family) for each function. Table 7.1 gives a sample listing and a suggested format for recording the methods–means analysis.

Must the System Analyst Summarize the Methods–Means Analysis?

After completing the system analysis, identifying performance requirements at each level, identifying possible methods–means solution vehicles of each, the analyst must prepare a methods–means summary to be used by the system designer during the system synthesis.

To make the summary, it is necessary to arrange performance requirements and the associated methods–means possibilities into functional families. Such families are related by the top-level function from which they derive and by subfunctions (derivative functions) that may be traced to the top-level functions. This methods–means summary provides the data base of performance requirements and associated possible methods and means for use in later selection of the methods and means.

How Are Methods–Means Obtained?

Do possible methods–means have to be in existence, or can they be identified so that we can "invent" new methods and/or means or synthesize old ones into new combinations? The goal is to accomplish the

TABLE 7.1   Sample Methods–Means Identification Form

Function	Performance Requirement	Methods–Means Possibilities	Advantages	Disadvantages
8.3.1	8.3.1—A Must provide signal return within 10 seconds	8.3.1A Ajax Model F	Available now	Not transportable
			Costs under $1,500	Reliability is .93
		8.3.1A Apex Model 10	Simple to use	Cost $2,700
		8.3.1A Contract for a special purpose device	Reliability of .997	Ready spring 1975
			Portable	Development and design costs of $10,800
	8.3.1–B Current school office staff must be able to use after reading an instruction book-let not to exceed ten pages so that there will be no more than 5 percent "down" time.	8.3.1–B Same as all 8.3.1–A M-Ms	Uses information sequenced by operation Reliability could be .999	Unit cost would reach 1,500 after 3,500 units delivered
	8.3.1–C Must operate within present school circuitry	8.3.1–C Same as all 8.3.1–A MMs	Portable Could be used for performance requirement 8.2.8.4	Ready summer 1976

mission with the greatest efficiency and effectiveness. If a method or a means does not exist and it seems probable that one could be invented or synthesized, then take the option as a possibility.[1] Progress through creative new efforts is important and can be a valuable product of a system approach. Reach, therefore, for the valid new idea and new methods–means.

Procedure for Performing Methods–Means Analysis

In performing a methods–means analysis, the following steps are recommended:

1. On the Methods–Means Identification form, record the function flow block diagram number of the function with which you are dealing.

1. It is well if an existing solution vehicle and strategy that are less efficient or otherwise "desirable" than the "inventable" one can serve as a safety back-up.

2. Under Performance Requirements, list the requirements that any methods–means combination must meet in order to be acceptable. Number these requirements alphanumerically to identify them with their appropriate functions.

3. Under Methods–Means Possibilities, list any methods–means combination meeting the requirements in the previous list. Number these to match the requirements list.

4. For each methods–means combination cited, list the advantages, such as availability, cost, time, reliability, transportability, and ease of use.

5. As in step 4, list all the known disadvantages for each methods–means combination cited.

6. Store the Methods–Means Analysis form with other associated functions. In a "large" analysis, you might require one file for each function in the mission profile.

7. Upon completion of the methods–means analysis (*at the task analysis level*) summarize the methods–means analysis into functional families as they relate to top-level (mission profile) functions or as they *might* relate with other functions from different top-level functions.

Confusing?

Doesn't this process of going from (1) functions and their performance requirements to (2) possible methods–means, to (3) constraints (if there are no possible methods–means combinations) become confusing? It might be so at first! But we are attempting to "capture" the process of system analysis. System analysis looks at the method–means derivation effort as "a system process model" and a way of learning how the parts *do* in fact go together. The description of what this process is and does may sound complicated. However, another look at the process shown diagrammatically in Fig. 7.2 should provide clarification.

The process of checking each function and the related performance requirements to see if there is a possible methods–means combination is essential. It will give assurance that on completion of analysis, the product will be an achievable product and will not result in the selection of some end-item or product which is not achievable. Thus the system designer can deal in realities and "achievements," not with dreams (or broken dreams) and unfulfilled promises.

The Methods–Means Analysis as a Feasibility Study

The methods–means analysis serves several crucial functions. First, it identifies the alternative possible methods and means (or strategies and tools) and lists the advantages and disadvantages of each for each performance requirement or group of performance requirements. Second, when used in an ongoing fashion as described in Fig. 7.4, it constitutes a feasibility study. A third function it serves is to force a consideration of alternatives for solving our problems, since we must list, whenever possible, at least two alternative methods–means for each performance requirement. These three features of a methods–means analysis deserve further discussion.

We have already noted that for each performance requirement (or family of related performance requirements) we list on a separate sheet the associated function number, the performance requirement(s) accompanying that particular function, and also the advantages and disadvantages for each identified possible methods–means combination. This listing provides a set of basic data for making the actual selection of methods and means at a later time.

Included and essential in any consideration of methods and means are the factors of time and cost. Of increasing usefulness in education today is a criterion called "cost benefit." Cost benefit is another way of asking the simple simultaneous questions of "What do I give?" and "What do I get?" During the system synthesis (especially step 3.0 in the generic educational problem-solving model—Fig. 2.1, page 12) we are going to use the system analysis information to select the most effective and efficient methods and means for meeting the identified needs. Of great importance in this decision will be the information we have gathered during the system analysis, especially the methods–means analysis.

Cost-Benefit Analysis

Cost-benefit analysis cannot be performed without the prior acquisition of certain data (so that the analyst may decide among the alternative methods and means identified in the methods–means analysis). When listing advantages and disadvantages, special attention should be devoted to the determination of variables and criteria that will be useful in the coming cost-benefit decision. It should be noted that cost benefit is not the same as cost efficiency—in functional education we are focusing on benefits (outcomes relating to documented needs); and the mere achievement of efficiency without benefits is a relatively shallow accomplishment. Thus in conducting the methods–means analysis it is particularly important to collect and list data concerning the time and cost dimensions as they relate to the performance requirements.

Because there is a constant determination of "what is to be done?" (the mission, function, and task analyses) and a determination of "can it be done?" (the methods–means analysis), we are conducting an ongoing feasibility study. The identification of a constraint—lack of a methods–

means for achieving a performance requirement—signals that there is a feasibility problem. When the constraint is reconciled, feasibility has been substantiated and the analysis continues. If a constraint cannot be reconciled, then the project (or at least one part of the project) is not feasible. This ongoing feasibility study assures us that, if and when we do complete task analysis and the methods–means analysis at a given level, we can in all probability meet the identified needs. We have identified all the requirements for problem resolution and have further identified the possible strategies and tools for meeting all requirements, including the listing of feasible alternative ways of getting the jobs done.

Requirements for Methods–Means Analysis

Creativity, innovation, and methods–means analysis should all go together. The suggestion that, for each performance requirement (or group of related performance requirements), there be at least two alternative methods–means listed, is an attempt to force the analyst to consider new and innovative possibilities. Frequently we are tempted to pick the solution vehicle with which we have the most familiarity and which has been successful in the past—an unfortunate tendency for true progress in better meeting the needs of learners. By formally considering the maximum likely number of methods–means alternatives, the analyst is encouraged to be bold, innovative, and creative. Indeed, innovativeness and creativity are encouraged by a system approach.

As the final step in performing an educational system analysis, it might be remembered that this step, like all the others, is designed only to identify "what" is to be done, not to select "how" to do it. In the case of methods–means analysis we are answering the following question: "What 'hows' are possible, and what are the advantages and disadvantages of each?"

All of system analysis as described here is concerned with educational system planning—by using it one is identifying both needs and requirements for meeting the needs; feasible alternatives for effective and efficient problem solving are also identified. The completion of the methods–means analysis signals that "what is to be done" has been accomplished; now "how to do it" may be determined, implemented, and evaluated. . . . And this is educational system planning.

Summary

Since the methods–means analysis relates to all the other steps of a system analysis, perhaps the best summary may be made diagrammatically (Fig. 7.3). A process chart summarizing the steps of system analysis appears in Fig. 7.4.

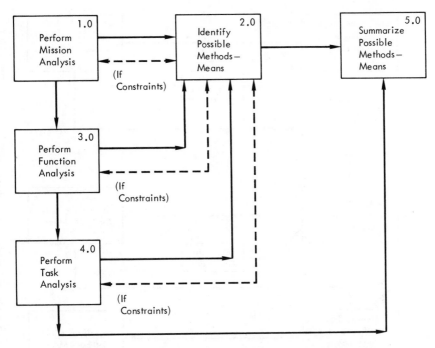

FIG. 7.3. The process for performing a methods–means analysis.

Glossary

Cost-benefit analysis: an analysis relating costs of a program (or an outcome) with the benefits to be accrued from the successful achievement of the outcomes. In its simplest form, cost-benefit analysis asks the two simultaneous questions of "What do I give?" and "What do I get?" There are tools for determining actual or predicted cost benefit, including the tools of "Planning–Programming–Budgeting System (PPBS)," and systems analysis (see Chapter 8).

Feasibility: capability of being carried out or completed successfully, with predicted success significantly greater than chance.

Exercises

1. Given a representative, valid task analysis derived from one function of a mission profile dealing with an educational problem, perform a methods–means analysis meeting the criteria for methods–means analysis as stated below:

1. All functions will be identified by a function flow block diagram numbering system.

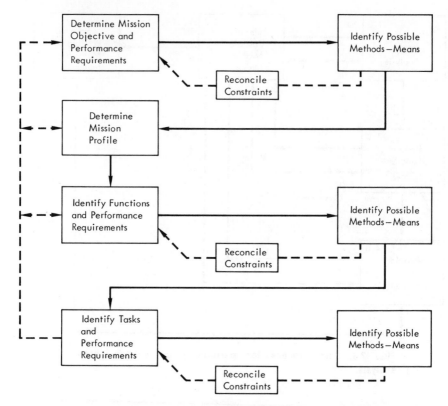

FIG. 7.4.   A system analysis process model that identifies the relation between the various steps in the process. Note that a continuous feasibility check is made during the process by identifying requirements in the mission, function, and task analyses and determining if there are any methods–means available for accomplishing each performance requirement or family of performance requirements. After R. Kaufman (1970a).

2. All performance requirements lists will contain those requirements specific to the function being analyzed and identified with that function alphanumerically.

3. All methods and means and possibilities cited will meet the performance requirements as set forth in step 2 and will be identified alphanumerically.

4. Each methods–means combination cited will be accompanied by specifications designating the advantages and disadvantages for its use.

For each function starting at 0.0, the mission objective and continuing down through at least one task, conduct a methods–means analysis at each level of analysis.

2. What is a method?

3. What is a means?

4. When is the methods–means analysis begun?

5. From what source does the methods–means information come?

6. What is the product of a methods–means analysis? What data does it contain?

7. How are the methods–means combinations identified?

8. There are seven basic steps in the performance of a methods–means analysis. List them.

doing what
you've planned

chapter 8

By this time you might be wondering what to do with all these boxes and arrows. Obviously a plan is not worthwhile unless it achieves predictable and relevant results.

Needs assessment and system analysis, as defined in this book, are tools for educational system planning. They cause us to start from a formal determination of educational needs (or gaps), which provides information concerning the needs with the highest priority for action. The discrepancy that is chosen to be acted upon then becomes the stated problem, and the mission analysis identifies the outcome specifications and a management plan (mission profile) for getting from where we are to where we should be. Function and task analyses provide us with detailed information concerning what is to be done to reach each element in the mission profile and the necessary interactions and interrelations among the various functions and tasks.

Finally, the methods–means analysis provides a feasibility determination that tells if (1) objectives are realizable and (2) possible alternative strategies and tools exist for achieving each of the many, many objectives required for problem solution.

At this point we have the answers to the following questions:

1. What are the needs?
2. What are the problems of highest priority?
3. What are the requirements to meet the needs and thus solve the problem(s)?
4. What are the possible strategies and tools to achieve the required performances, and what are the advantages and disadvantages of each?

Thus we have identified all the feasible "whats" for problem solution. Referring to the six-step process model of a system approach, which by this time is quite familiar, we have completed the first two functions: 1.0, identify problem based on needs and 2.0, determine solution requirements and alternatives. We would now be ready for the "synthesis" portion of a system approach, and we have the necessary information to act with assurance that we would meet the high-priority identified needs. Thus educational system planning (as defined here) is accomplished, and we may proceed to system synthesis.

Following is a very brief description of system synthesis to serve as a preliminary guide for those who want to go past system planning to system accomplishment.

Selecting Solution Strategies from Among Alternatives

As a result of the methods–means analysis, we know the possible strategies and vehicles for achieving each performance requirement and the relative advantages and disadvantages of each. Based on this information, the designer is to select the best alternatives (function 3.0 in the generic system approach process model). This can be a messy job.

Methods–means selection is frequently made by hunches and intuition, with the likelihood that the latest gimmick or the most comfortable solution will be picked. Now, new and useful techniques are available. Furthermore, new techniques of deciding among alternative solutions have been developing for several years—tools such as systems analysis, cost-benefit analysis, and the like. Several accounts are available detailing procedures for making these kinds of determinations, including two books by Cleland and King (1968, 1969).

In a rather complete discussion of tools that seem to be of greatest value when applied to the generic function of "select solution strategies from among alternatives," Alkin and Bruno (1970) discuss a number of procedures and tools which they relate to "systems approaches." These include: operations research, planning–programming–budgeting systems (PPBS); systems analysis; and "other system analytic techniques," including simulations, operational gaming, the Delphi technique, the program evaluation review technique (PERT), and the critical path method (CPM). Building on Alkin and Bruno's delineation, capsule summaries of operations research, PPBS, system analysis, simulations, and operational gaming are presented below, primarily to let the reader know of their existence and to encourage more reading where individual situations call for synthesis-type activities.

Operations Research

According to Alkin and Bruno (1970), operations research

... may be considered a method of obtaining optimum solutions to problems in which relationships are specified and criteria for evaluating effectiveness are known. Operations research summarizes alternatives into mathematical expressions and models. It then identifies the set of alternatives that maximizes or minimizes the desired criterion for evaluating effectiveness.

It might be concluded, then, that operations research as defined in this manner has potential but perhaps no immediate usefulness to educational implementation until the goals, objectives, and requirements for educational accomplishment have been determined and are in a form that allows for quantification. If viable educational system planning is accomplished using the tools of needs assessment and system analysis, however, operations research could be of significant utility.

Planning–Programming–Budgeting Systems

Most discussions of PPBS note that as a tool it is best used for taking the objectives of education, identifying alternative courses of action intended to meet the objectives (including a determination of costs and benefits associated with each), and ranking the various alternative choices (sometimes called "systems") in terms of their respective costs and benefits; then choices among the alternatives may be made on a more rational and empirical basis, and it is possible to derive a budget based on cost of achieving objectives.

The utility of PPBS would seem to depend greatly on the validity of the original objectives chosen for further study and evaluation.

Systems Analysis

The technique of systems analysis as defined by Cleland and King (1968) is different from the definition of system analysis as described in previous chapters (cf. Kaufman, 1970). Cleland and King define this tool as:

1. Systematic examination and comparison of those alternative actions which are related to the accomplishment of desired objectives.

2. Comparisons of alternatives on the basis of the resource cost and the benefit associated with each alternative.

3. Explicit consideration of uncertainty.

Conceived in this manner, systems analysis is most useful when we have in fact identified objectives and requirements based on needs and are ready to locate and consider possible alternative methods and means. Thus conceived, systems analysis would be most advantageously applied after the completion of educational system planning, and thus when objectives have been derived from a needs assessment and system analysis.

Other tools may also be of assistance in the selection of methods and means (and perhaps also applicable in the next system approach step of implementation): simulation and operational gaming.

Simulation

Simulation is simply building and using a model of a real or predicted event or situation. It can vary from a physical mock-up of a building or a classroom to see "how it will work" in practice to quite complex, mathematical models with multiple interacting variables.

Suppose we want to know how well a school layout, selected from among our identified alternative methods–means, might work. We could build a miniature model of it and attempt to extrapolate its usefulness and problems in order to help "predict" its effectiveness and efficiency.

Operational Gaming

A variation of simulation (and other types of model building), operational gaming tends to use human beings playing roles in a given context or situation. For instance, if we were facing a major school board meeting at which several methods for raising additional funds for the schools would be discussed, we might decide to "role-play" the situation: each person would assume the character of a board member and the meeting could be predictively "created" to determine what might happen at the actual event.

Operational gaming, and simulation, too, may be used at any time during the implementation phase. A manager might want to carry out a simulation or game before taking a specified and previously planned action to test whether it will in fact yield the desired outcome. By so doing, he would have the opportunity to change his approach to implementation or even revise his methods and means, if necessary.

Summary of Alternatives

These alternative techniques provide the educator with methods and procedures by which the most effective and efficient strategies and tools may be determined to meet the needs and requirements derived during the system planning phase (functions 1.0 and 2.0). They all tend to relate to the questions of cost benefit and cost effectiveness, which is another way of answering the two simultaneous questions of "What do I get?" and "What do I give?" Obviously, one wants to make available the best learning conditions for the least expenditure, and such tools as those just described will help to achieve that end.

Implementation

Implementation is the actual doing of what was planned, using the selected tools and strategies. When dealing with curriculum, the materials are made, purchased, or otherwise obtained, tried out on a target population typical of the one for which they are intended, and revised. When dealing with educational support, people are hired and/or trained, and the like.

Implementation is what educators do best, since we have been rewarded most of our lives for doing things, but we receive little stimulative encouragement for planning. Implementation can be managed and controlled so that required outcomes are achieved. Of significant utility in implementation is a management and control tool called PERT (Program Evaluation Review Technique) and its close relative CPM (Critical Path Method), which are time-line, sequential graphic representations of milestones or events. These network-based management tools provide the implementer with information concerning what has to be done, when it has to be done, and what happens to everything else if one element of a plan is either early or late. Cook (1966, 1967) provides excellent expositions on network-based management tools. The data from a system analysis (and especially the task analysis) have great utility as the primary input into PERT or CPM.

Determination of Performance Effectiveness

How well or how poorly the needs have been met defines performance effectiveness. A number of tools are available aside from those relatively comfortable norm-referenced testing instruments. Criterion-referenced testing (Glaser, 1966) is useful for accomplishing the function of valid determination of outcome. Other tools include, but are not limited to, national assessment as a vehicle for determining what is known by representative members of our educational charges (if we want to know about the "big" picture), and a tool relatively new to education, which is related to, but different from evaluation—the independent educational accomplishment audit (Lessinger, 1970). An auditor determines the extent to which a planner has accomplished his objectives, using the data of expenditures of time and money much the same way a certified public accountant audits a commercial organization. Usually evaluation at this stage of system design and development is of the summative variety and tells us about the extent to which we did or did not meet the objectives that were derived from the documented needs.

Revising as Required

Revision not only happens last, it is also continuous and ongoing. It relates to the concept of formative evaluation (see p. 140), whereby any time the interim or in-process objectives are not being met, necessary revisions may be made. This self-correctional feature is the element which assures that the needs will be eventually met. It also provides educators with the right to fail *and* the ultimate obligation to succeed—new and boldly creative things may be tried; and if these are found wanting, new and more responsive techniques may be substituted. We may fail frequently, but the most important ultimate criterion is whether we did the job.

The critical tool involved in revision is the requirement that the process information be systematically and periodically reported to the decision maker so that necessary corrective action may be taken. It is also important to recall that the revise-as-required step is to take place throughout system planning and implementation. Using this "formative" evaluation, there is a constant check on utility and an attempt to make the system responsive. Thus the approach is not a rigid, unyielding experiment, but rather a "people-centered," flexible process for meeting human needs.

In summary, there are a number of tools that take us from the planning of successful education outcomes to their actual achievement. These tools are not covered in detail here, for the several referenced resources (plus many others) for these tools will allow the planner to make the transition to "doer." Fig. 8.1 shows a possible relation between some planning tools, some synthesis tools, and the suggested system approach process model.

If educational system planning, including needs assessment and system analysis, is only the beginning of the educational enterprise, it is the critical step in assuring that relevant and practical solutions will be identified, selected, and applied to real problems. It also is the first step in educational accountability—being responsible for what we are charged with accomplishing. It provides the criteria for a reasonable accountability, based on at least the following elements:

1. Real needs.

2. A co-commitment regarding the exact nature of the expected outcomes from the partners in education (learners, community, and educators).

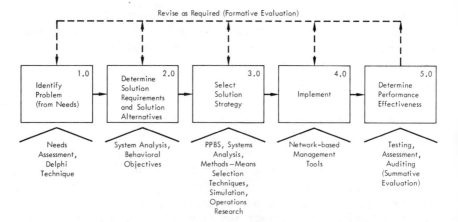

FIG. 8.1. Possible relation between current tools for the improvement of education and their relation to a problem-solving process model (system approach). After Kaufman (1971a, 1971b).

3. A shared responsibility for the outcomes between the partners —each partner knows and agrees on his precise responsibility for contributing and achieving.

The suggested system approach process model and its associated tools and procedures form a basic process (and a type of logic or thinking) for defining and achieving a realistic educational responsibility and accountability.

By using it, means and ends will be placed in more proper perspective, and the utilization of means will be based not upon whim or fancy, but upon its probability of meeting high priority needs.

Glossary

Criterion-referenced item: a test or evaluation item referring to a specific behavior or performance ideally derived from a needs assessment and system analysis. It provides a realistic alternative to "norm-referenced" test items.

Formative evaluation: the determination of "in-process" or on-going activities and results, including a determination of the extent to which processes and procedures are working or have worked in meeting overall objectives and requirements. It also supplies criteria for in-process changes in an operating system.

Operational gaming: a variation of simulation usually characterized by the assumption of roles by people in a given (hypothetical) context or situation.

Operations research: a method of obtaining optimum solutions to problems in which criteria and interrelationships are well defined, usually being expressed in mathematical models.

Program Evaluation Review Technique: PERT—one of several network-based tools for planning the implementation of an educational system. These tools, including CPM (Critical Path Method), are time-line, sequential graphic representations of milestones or events which can show the consequences of changes in implementation activities, including changes in the categories dollars, time, and resources.

Simulation: the building and using of a model of a real or predicted event or situation.

Summative evaluation: the customary mode of educational evaluation, wherein final outcomes or results are determined.

Systems analysis: a tool for the selection of the most effective and efficient alternative actions based on alternative resource cost and benefit and a consideration of uncertainty.

Exercises

1. What will result from conducting a needs assessment and a system analysis?

2. List the steps of a system approach that are primarily concerned with "doing," or system synthesis.

3. As used in this book, what is the relation between "system analysis" and "systems analysis?"

4. Define the following terms and state where each is used in a system approach.

    a. Summative evaluation.

    b. Formative evaluation.

planning
what you do

chapter 9

Getting Started in System Planning

The material of this book is but a first step in educational system planning. It described the tools, techniques, and concepts of planning, using two key instruments—needs assessment and system analysis.

The first requisite for successful educational system planning is obtaining the commitment to planning. This requires a shift from the customary reaction to situational crises to the deliberate identification of needs and the systematic process of naming goals and requirements and meeting them in an effective and efficient manner. The commitment to educational planning should be made by all the educational partners on the basis of wanting to achieve relevant and practical education using precise techniques and methods. A requirement to plan will not be successful unless all members accept it.

Next is a commitment to the tools of planning, especially needs assessment and system analysis. Both a consideration of what the tools are designed to accomplish and a comparison with alternative planning methods are required. The planning tools should be selected on the deliberate rationale that they *will* supply the information required to achieve successful implementation.

Assuming that the tools of needs assessment and system analysis have been accepted, members of the planning team should become proficient in the use of the tools; the alternative is to delegate the responsibility for use of the tools to team members in whom the others have confidence. It should be noted that although not all people find it easy to learn system analysis, it is basically a simple tool—so simple in fact that it could probably be successfully taught to elementary school children so that it could become a fundamental aid for them in education and in life.

Methods of instruction, however, will vary according to the learning styles of individuals and the type of planning required.

The planning should take place in an open and constructively critical environment. The purpose of the tools is to supply information that will result in sensible, sensitive, and responsive decisions relating to learning and learners. Planning provides a communication tool and a communication referent, and it is up to all the partners to review and improve the planning data.

Finally there is the commitment to use the information that comes from formal educational system planning. Situational crises, expediency, or "hidden agenda" groups and forces must not be allowed to sidetrack or deflect the implementation of the plan—the only things that should change the plan are empirical data concerning its viability, or lack of it. The system approach process should be used for planning and implementation, since it furnishes a systematic and logical process for identifying and resolving educational problems.

Evaluation and Revision—Keys to Self-Renewal, Relevancy, and Responsiveness

In a system approach, each function and task has potential interaction with every other function and task; and when each one has reached the successive stages of planning and implementation, the extent to which each has or has not been accomplished must be ascertained and evaluated. Thus in a system approach constant evaluation, decision making, and possible revision are of critical importance to the successful meeting of needs.

Evaluation and revision are central to self-renewal and to relevancy. If the revision that is required is not made, then there exists a potential "galloping system," which is operating out of control. A self-correcting (or perhaps better, continually correcting) system is constantly asking, "How well has it been done?", "Are we doing what we set out to do?", "How can we do it better?", and "Is this what we should be doing?" This evaluation and self-correction feature appears in the system approach process model as it relates to the dotted lines in the flow chart—it says "revise as required." Notice that the dotted line does provide the opportunity for each function to interact with every other function. Notice also that the feedback (or revision) route includes the very first function— namely, "identify problem based upon needs." To attain responsiveness, the starting point for system planning and design—the needs—are always being questioned, revised, updated, corrected, or discarded. By so doing, we better assure that we remain relevant and that we renew our plans and programs on the basis of current documented needs.

Evaluation: Evaluation is used here as the determination of the extent to which you have accomplished that which you set out to accomplish. Harsh (in Chenney, Harsh, Kaufman, Shuck, and Wood, 1970) states that evaluation "is concerned with the determination of what's being or been accomplished." He further points out that:

> *...historically, in education, focus of evaluation has been upon outcomes (or products, or ends) and there has been a tendency to neglect determination of the utility of the process for achieving required outcomes.*

It is necessary, therefore, to determine the extent to which planning has achieved required results *and* to determine the degree to which the processes selected and utilized have contributed or are contributing to the achievement of the required outcomes. Continuing, Harsh refers to the two types of evaluation as being formative evaluation and summative evaluation. *Formative evaluation* is concerned with the determination of the utility of processes and procedures for achieving the outcomes, and *summative evaluation* is concerned with the extent of achievement of the outcomes.

Summative Evaluation: Summative evaluation is a determination of the degree to which we have accomplished our ends; thus the "hard" criteria derived from a formal needs assessment and system analysis provide us with several things:

> 1. Assurance that what we are measuring not only has a high probability of being valid (since there has been a formal determination of what is required in the "real world"), but it has based the requirements for outcomes on this "real world" state of affairs.
> 2. Assurance that there are viable, measurable criteria for evaluation.

The summative evaluation is best when it measures that which is of importance, and the possibility of taking evaluation criteria directly from the data supplied in a needs assessment and system analysis yields additional assurance. Instruments for summative evaluation are shifting from the older and more comfortable "norm-referenced" tests to the more specific and useful "criterion-referenced" testing instruments. The best criterion-referenced test items have their roots in data from the actual environment for which we are preparing our learners.

Formative evaluation: Again referring to Harsh (Chenney, Harsh, Kaufman, Shuck, and Wood, 1970):

> *In contrast to summative evaluation where no changes in definition
> of objectives, methods, or assessments are appropriate,
> formative evaluation (if it is to be a service to development) is
> designed to monitor the changes that occur in development; and,
> as the data are fed back to the planners and developers and new
> objectives are stated or methods are used, the assessments and
> data-gathering procedures will be modified to accurately reflect
> the developments from that point forward.*

Thus formative evaluation provides information relative to whether we are "on target," and if we are not, it gives information for midcourse corrections to assure that we will eventually be successful.

Both summative and formative evaluation are directly related to and involved in planning and accomplishment. If the objectives for summative evaluation are to be valid, they must be based on correct information; and this is provided by a properly executed needs assessment and system analysis. Planning stems from these objectives based on documented and defined needs. While the plan itself is being accomplished, formative evaluation will serve to provide the educational designer and manager with correct information on necessary changes; finally, it will tell them what they *should* know about the utility of the various processes selected and utilized to achieve the stated goals.

Revision: Revision is change stimulated by performance data that indicate where modifications should be made to meet the identified needs and associated requirements. The nature of the changes is indicated, too, although revision is not *just* redoing for its own sake—it is the logical and planned modification or replacement of previous functions and tasks. Revision is easier to accomplish during planning than during implementation. The whole planning process is designed to provide an open divulgence of the plan, the components, and their interrelations; and modifications are usually a part of the planning process. During implementation, however, numerous commitments of people and facilities have already been made, and there may be vested interests in one or more parts of a committed plan.

Since the notion of planning implies that we cannot predict the future with complete certainty, it should not be surprising to find that even the best plans require constant revision. Of course, the "better" the plan, the fewer the revisions; but reality and experience tell us that there is no such thing as a perfect plan.

Whenever a revision is made, it should be carefully verified that all the interactions (or consequences) of the change have also been accounted for—a type of "replanning." Remember that any change in a dynamic system has implications for all the other parts. The constant evaluation and revision demanded in a system approach are the price of relevancy and self-renewal. An unyielding and unchanging program will not retain its viability in a changing world where constant sensitivity to the needs of people is essential.

Responsiveness: The fact that a system approach requires constant evaluation and revision whenever the individual requirements are not being met makes it a responsive and humanistic approach. Formative evaluation and the ability to change in "mid-stream" differentiate a system approach from more rigid and tidy approaches generally associated with the tools and techniques of experimental psychology and physics.

Toward a Possible Taxonomy of Educational Planning

We still might ask, "Well, what really *is* planning?" Some say that PERT is planning; others say PPBS, system analysis, or systems analysis are planning. Following is a possible way to sort and order many of the currently applied tools differentially termed or associated with "planning" (Kaufman, 1970a).

Each of the functions shown in the system approach model can be accomplished by applying the six-step problem-solving process to the functions individually. For instance, to perform the first function ("identify problem based on needs") we can go through the six steps for that function alone. In turn, we may apply the same generic process to each other step. This being the case, there is a requirement for planning in each of the six steps in the generic process, since each one presents a gap between the current situation and the required situation—the accomplishment of that unique function.

Continuing with this logic, it is perfectly possible for an educator to start planning at any one of the six steps identified in the generic process if he is willing to *assume* that the previous steps have been accomplished or if the data produced by the preceding steps are in fact available. For example, we could start planning and doing at the third step if we assume that the needs assessment has been completed and that the system analysis data were also available, or if we have the data in hand. (In actual educational practice unfortunately, planning and doing frequently start at the third or fourth function in the generic process, without the accomplishment of the previous functions.)

It is not surprising, therefore, to find that a number of tools have been identified as relating to planning: needs assessment, system analysis, PPBS, systems analysis, PERT, CPM, and the like—they all *are* concerned with planning! The distinction between these tools might well lie in the extent to which they depend, either in fact or by assumption, on the data from previous planning and accomplishment.

It is suggested, therefore, that there exists a possible taxonomy of planning—each subsequent planning tool depending on the data from preceding efforts. It is further suggested that there are at least six kinds of planning, with their distinctive tools, which are best when associated with the performance of the required functions characterized by each of the six steps in the generic problem-solving process (Kaufman, 1971a):

Alpha planning: identify problem based on needs.

Beta planning: determine solution requirements and solution alternatives.

Gamma planning: select solution strategies from among alternatives.

Delta planning: implement.

Epsilon planning: determine performance effectiveness.

Zeta planning: revise as required.

Tools associated with each type of planning could be:

Alpha planning: needs assessment, Delphi technique.

Beta planning: system analysis (and possibly resulting performance objectives).

Gamma planning: PPBS, systems analysis, simulation, operations research.

Delta planning: PERT, CPM, other network-based management tools.

Epsilon planning: experimental design, summative evaluation techniques, auditing.

Zeta planning: formative evaluation.

If this formulation works, a matrix may be developed to identify possible tools (and gaps) associated with the successful planning and implementation of educational systems. Such a matrix could have the six system process model steps as the abscissa and the types of planning as the ordinate. (Like most concepts, this one requires further study, development, revision, or junking.)

Toward Increased Precision in Stating and Using Goals and Objectives

Almost everyone in educational agencies today is talking about (and occasionally using) goals, objectives, aims, and purposes as part of the daily routine. One thing seems to be certain, only the operational charac-

teristics and features of measurable, performance objectives are relatively clear. It ought to be useful for the educational planner and implementer if some logical and useful distinction could be made among these
terms. Following is a possible taxonomy for outcomes.

A Possible Taxonomy of Educational Outcomes

S. S. Stevens, in his chapter "Mathematics, Measurement, and
Psychophysics" in the landmark *Handbook of Experimental Psychology*
(1951) reminded us of different scales of measurement, which range from
nominal scales to the most precise ratio scales. His listing of scales of
measurement appears as Table 8.1.

It is suggested that the terms goal, aim, purpose, and objective may
relate to Stevens's scale properties as follows:

Scale of measurement	Outcome descriptor
Nominal Ordinal	Goal, aim, purpose
Interval Ratio	Objectives (measurable, performance, or behavioral)

Thus there is nothing to say that, when we speak of "goals," for
instance, these are not useful to us; it is only that they do not contain as
much "information" in terms of their underlying properties of measurement as would a "measurable objective." The difference between goals,
aims, and purposes as distinct from "objectives" is thus a difference of
degree rather than of kind. The more information there is in an outcome
statement, the greater our ability to use the goals, and so on for educational design—precision and measurability are critical to the success of
educational system planning.

A further possibility exists if this formulation is correct; then evaluation validity might well be tied to the form and properties of the data
upon which an evaluation is based. For instance, if we make a decision
on the basis of nominal data, we might be risking more (our predicted
validity is lower) than if we had ordinal data; and this in turn would be
more "risky" than if we had interval data. Finally, the greatest predicted
validity would be attached to a situation in which we were fortunate
enough to acquire educational data that had ratio scale properties. Thus
the validity of a decision might be related to the measurement scale
properties of the data used in the decision-making process,[1] and this

---

1. *It is further tempting to hypothesize that behavior often characterized
as "biased" or "prejudiced" could be associated with a decision made on the
basis of nominal or ordinal data but with the imputation, inference (or even
belief) that it really was based on interval or ratio data.*

TABLE 8.1 Scales of Measurement

The basic operations needed to create a given scale are all those listed in the second column, down to and including the operation listed opposite the scale. The third column gives the mathematical transformations that leave the scale form invariant. Any numeral x on a scale can be replaced by another numeral x', where x' is the function of x listed in column 3. The fourth column lists, cumulatively downward, some of the statistics that show invariance under the transformations of column 3.

Scale	Basic Empirical Operations	Mathematical Group Structure	Permissible Statistics (invariantive)	Typical Examples
Nominal	Determination of equality	Permutation group $x' = f(x)$ [$f(x)$ means any one-to-one substitution]	Number of cases Mode Contingency correlation	"Numbering" of football players Assignment of type or model numbers to classes
Ordinal	Determination of greater or less	Isotonic group $x' = f(x)$ [$f(x)$ means any increasing monotonic function]	Median Percentiles Order correlation (type O)	Hardness of minerals Quality of leather, lumber, wool, etc. Pleasantness of odors
Interval	Determination of equality of intervals or differences	General linear group $x' = ax + b$	Mean Standard deviation Order correlation (type I) Product-moment correlation	Temperature (Fahrenheit and centigrade) Energy Calendar dates "Standard scores" on achievement tests (?)
Ratio	Determination of equality of ratios	Similarity group $x' = ax$	Geometric mean Coefficient of variation Decibel transformations	Length, weight, density, resistance, etc. Pitch scale (mels) Loudness scale (sones)

From S.S. Stevens, "Mathematics, Measurement, and Psychophysics," in S.S. Stevens, ed., *Handbook of Experimental Psychology* (New York: John Wiley, 1962).

formulation might help clear up some of the current muddle generated by some in the field who confuse "bad" evaluation (generalizing past the data) with *all* evaluation. "Silly" evaluation might well be the case when one has nominal or ordinal data and attempts to use interval or ratio instruments, or the converse, if one has interval or ratio data and attempts to use nominal or ordinal evaluation instruments. With this model, evaluation may be made using nominal, ordinal, interval, or ratio data—it is suggested, however, that the greater the precision and reliability of the data, the higher the probability of a valid decision.[2]

But precision and reliability of underlying data alone *is not enough* to assure validity, for we could make very wrong decisions, very measurably, very precisely, if some of our basic assumptions and starting points were incorrect. In order for system analysis (or any model) to be satisfactory, it is of critical importance that any measurability be realistic. It is for this reason that the starting point for any measurement, evaluation, design, or decision must be with the individual person and his needs and the needs of his partners. Measurement for its own sake is counterproductive. Measurement related to the extent of our responsiveness to individuals is imperative if we are to provide educational opportunities responsibly, realistically, and sensitively. This is why this book has put so much emphasis on starting educational activities with a formal assessment of needs before proceeding with a systematic planning and doing effort.

It should be emphasized that the previous two concepts are indeed preliminary and tentative in nature and are presented only for consideration. More analysis and validation are necessary before further use can be recommended. The attempt is to define and quantify more thoroughly those factors in education which might lead us to better planning and successful implementation, and increased precision is a good starting place.

These formulations, including those of needs assessment, a system approach, and system analysis, are all indeed crude and preliminary; and they await the scrutiny of responsible professional educators for the ultimate determination of their worth.

A system approach is a holistic approach. By formally attempting to consider the nuances of human behavior, the known interaction of human performance and characteristics, and the complexities of the interactions and interrelationships which are important, the job might at first seem overwhelming. This book has attempted to supply some tools, techniques, and logic for planning an effective, efficient, and individually responsive educational enterprise. To consider less would result in a dehumanization which would be intolerable to most responsible people.

Hopefully, the foregoing content will be considered by those who want to make a difference for learners, and applied, revised, or replaced in a system manner to achieve a world where every person is mindful of the rights and responsibilities of himself and others in a systematic and purposive way.

---

2. *There also might be some basic philosophical and psychological relations between the modes of operation and decision making using the different measurement scales. We might call decisions based on nominal or ordinal data "value judgments" and those based on interval or ratio data "logical" or "rational."*

Exercises

1. Following are the six steps for the system approach process; for each item, list at least one tool that could be used for its accomplishment:

    a. Identify problem (based on needs).

    b. Determine solution requirements and solution alternatives.

    c. Select solution strategies from among alternatives.

    d. Implement.

    e. Determine performance effectiveness.

    f. Revise as required.

2. Name the type of planning represented by each of the following examples:

    a. Implement differentiated staffing.

    b. Determine the most effective and efficient method for individualizing instruction.

    c. Determine the effectiveness of a new science program.

    d. By June 4, 90 percent of all learners in the first grade at Sierra School will be reading at or above grade level.

3. According to the formulation concerning a possible taxonomy of educational outcomes, list the scale type for each of the following statements:

    a. Blue-eyed dogs are lazy.

    b. Today is Tuesday.

    c. John is three inches shorter than Juan.

    d. The weather report at 2:30 P.M. states that it is 14 degrees cooler today than it was yesterday at the same time.

    e. Stockley won second prize in a male beauty contest yesterday, and thus he is better-looking than George, who got fourth prize.

    f. We want to improve reading skills.

    g. Prepare objectives in the affective domain.

    h. By September 24, all children in the kindergarten class at Blau Elementary School will be able to complete a traffic safety test developed by the Parent-Teachers Association and approved by the city traffic division. The children will then be able to cross at intersections and obey traffic laws, and during the school year there should be no more than one reported case per month of safety violations by a registered learner made to the school by the city police or safety patrol in the school.

i.   Improve self-concept.

j.   Develop each child to his own capacity.

4.   List the five greatest disadvantages of conducting educational system planning.

5.   List the five greatest advantages of conducting educational system planning.

6.   In what ways could this book on educational system planning be improved?

7.   What modifications to the system approach process presented in this book should be made?

8.   Conduct a needs assessment and a system analysis for an educational problem. Implement it, and determine the effectiveness of educational system planning.

bibliography

THE ALABAMA STATE DEPARTMENT OF EDUCATION, "A Study of Educational Needs in Alabama Schools." Montgomery, Ala., April, 1969.

ALKIN, M. C., and J. E. BRUNO, "System Approaches to Educational Planning," Part IV of *Social and Technological Change: Implications for Education.* ERIC/CEA, University of Oregon, Eugene, 1970.

ATKINSON, R. C., "Computerized Instruction and the Learning Process," *American Psychologist*, April, 1968.

AXTELLE, G. E., "The Humanizing of Knowledge and the Education of Values," *Educational Theory*, XVI No. 2 (April, 1966).

BANATHY, B. H., *Instructional Systems.* Palo Alto, Calif.: Fearon Publishers, Inc., 1968.

BARRO, S. M., "An Approach to Developing Accountability Measures for the Public Schools" *Phi Delta Kappan*, Vol. LII, No. 4, December, 1970.

BARSON, J., and R. HEINICH, "A Systems Approach," *Audiovisual Instruction* June, 1966.

———, and E. K. OXHANDLER, "Systems: An Approach to Improving Instruction," *Audiovisual Instruction*, May, 1965.

BAY, D. L., P. P. PREISING, and A. DE JONG, "1968 Needs Assessment." Supplementary Education Center, San Jose, Calif., 1968.

BEALS, R. L., "Resistance and Adaptation to Technological Change: Some Anthropological Views," *Human Factors*, December, 1968.

BELLIOTT, F. K., "Design for Tennessee Assessment and Evaluation of Title III, E.S.E.A." State of Tennessee Department of Education, March 31, 1969.

BENYEI, P., and J. GILKEY, "The Instructional Unit—A Systems Approach to Multimedia," *Audiovisual Instruction*, XV, No. 1 (January, 1970).

BERN, H. A., "Audiovisual Engineers?" *AV Communication Review*, IX, No. 4 (July–August, 1961).

———, "Wanted: Educational Engineers," *Phi Delta Kappan*, January, 1967.

BLOOD, R. E., G. I. BROWN, D. L. BRUBAKER, and R. M. THOMAS, "The Study of Unmet Educational Needs: A Discrepancy-Score Approach." Tri-County Supplementary Educational Service Center, Santa Barbara, Calif., undated.

BLOOM, B. S., J. T. HASTINGS, and G. F. MADAUS, *Handbook on Formative and Summative Evaluation of Student Learning.* New York: McGraw-Hill Book Company, 1971.

BRAIN, G. B., "What's the Score on National Assessment?" *California Teachers Association Journal*, May, 1969.

BRICKELL, H. M., "Organizing New York State for Educational Change." New York State Department of Education, Albany, N. Y., December, 1961.

BRIGGS, L. J., ET AL., *Instructional Media: A Procedure for the Design of Multi-Media Instruction.* American Institutes for Research, Pittsburgh, Pa., 1967.

————, and G. K. TALLMADGE, *Plan of Action to be Followed by Contractors in Developing Each of Four Proposed Multi-Media Courses of Instruction for the U. S. Naval Academy.* American Institutes for Research AIR-F-63-2/67FR, Pittsburgh, Pa., March 6, 1967.

BROOKS, C. N., "Training System Evaluation Using Mathematical Models," *Educational Technology*, June, 1969.

BUCKLEY, W. (ed.), *Modern Systems Research for the Behavioral Scientist.* Chicago, Ill.: Aldine Publishing Company, 1968.

CARLSON, RICHARD O., *Adoption of Educational Innovations.* Center for the Advanced Study of Educational Administration, University of Oregon, Eugene, August, 1965.

CARPENTER, C. R., "New Teaching Aids for the American Classroom" (Wilbur Schramm, ed.), Institute for Communications Research, Stanford University, 1960. Also reprinted by U.S. Department of Health, Education, and Welfare, E-34020, 1962.

CARPENTER, M. B., "Program Budgeting as a Way to Clarify Issues in Education," RAND Corporation, July, 1968.

CARTER, L. F., "The Systems Approach to Education—The Mystique and the Reality," System Development Corporation, Rept. SP-3291, January 27, 1969.

————, and H. SILBERMAN, "The System Approach, Technology and the School," System Development Corporation, SP-2025, 1965.

CHARTERS, W. W., "Is There a Field of Educational Engineering?" *Educational Bulletin*, Ohio State University, 1954.

CHENNEY, E. M., J. R. HARSH, R. A. KAUFMAN, L. E. SHUCK, and R. R. WOOD, *A Plan For Planning.* Inglewood Unified School District, Inglewood, Calif., August, 1970.

CHURCHMAN, C. W., *The Systems Approach.* New York: Dell Publishing Company, Inc., 1969.

CLARK, J. W. (ed.), "Systems Education Patterns on the Drawing Boards for the Future," in *Highlights of the Second Annual National Conference on General Systems Education.* Cheshire, Conn., November 1, 1968.

CLELAND, D. I., and W. R. KING, *Systems Analysis and Project Management.* New York: McGraw-Hill Book Company, 1968.

————, *Systems, Organizations, Analysis, Management: A Book of Readings.* New York: McGraw-Hill Book Company, 1969.

COGSWELL, J. F., "System Technology in Education," in J. W. Loughary, et al., *Man–Machine Systems in Education.* New York: Harper & Row, Publishers, 1966.

CONSULTING SERVICES CORPORATION, "Washington State Student Needs Assessment." Seattle, Wash., March, 1969.

COOK, D. L., *PERT: Applications in Education*, OE-1214, Cooperative Research Monogr. No. 17. Washington, D.C.: Government Printing Office, 1966.

————, "Better Project Planning and Control Through the Use of System Analysis and Management Techniques," paper presented at Operations Analysis of Education Symposium, Washington, D.C., November 1967.

————, "An Overview of Management Science in Educational Research," a paper presented to the Symposium on Management Science in Educational Research, Cleveland, Ohio, September, 1968a. Educational Program Management Center, Ohio State University.

————, "A Generalized Project Management System Model," Educational Program Management Center, Ohio State University, November, 1968b.

————, "Management Control Theory as the Context for Educational Evaluation" (prepublication draft). Educational Program Management Center, College of Education, Ohio State University, final draft, April 1, 1970.

CORRIGAN, R. E., "The Development of Group Tutorial Instructional Methods at Alamitos School District." Garden Grove, Calif., undated.

————, "Method–Media Selection," OPERATION PEP. Tulare County (Calif.), Department of Education, 1965.

————, "Programmed Instruction as a Systems Approach to Education," in G. Ofiesh, and W. C. Meierhenry, *Trends in Programmed Instruction.* National Society for Programmed Instruction and National Education Association Department of Audiovisual Instruction, Washington, D.C., 1966a.

————, "System Cost/Effectiveness Criteria or Selecting the Proper Resources and Plans to Achieve Stated Mission Objectives," OPERATION PEP. Tulare County (Calif.) Department of Education, 1966b.

————, Associates, *A System Approach for Education (SAFE).* R. E. Corrigan Associates: Garden Grove, Calif., 1969.

————, BETTY O. CORRIGAN, and R. A. KAUFMAN, "The Steps and Tools of the System Synthesis Process in Education," OPERATION PEP. San Mateo County (Calif.) Department of Education, December, 1967.

————, and D. W. JOHNSON, "The Requirements and Process for Planned Educational Change: State of California," OPERATION PEP. Tulare County (Calif.) Department of Education, 1966.

————, and R. A. KAUFMAN, *Why System Engineering?* Palo Alto, Calif.: Fearon Publishers, Inc., 1966.

CRUMBAUGH, J. C., and L. T. MAHOLICK, *Manual of Instructions for the Purpose in Life Test.* Brookport, Ill.: Psychometric Affiliates, 1969.

CYPHERT, F. R., and W. L. GANT, "The Delphi Technique: A Case Study," *Phi Delta Kappan*, LII, No. 5 (January, 1971).

CYRES, T. E., JR., and RITA LOWENTHAL, "A Model for Curriculum Design Using a Systems Approach," *Audiovisual Instruction*, XV, No. 1 (January, 1970).

DALKEY, N., "Use of the Delphi Technique in Educational Planning," Sacramento, Calif.: *Educational Resources Agency Herald*, IV, No. 2 (November–December, 1970).

DUBIN, R., and T. C. TAVEGGIA, *The Teaching-Learning Paradox*. Center for the Advanced Study of Educational Administration, University of Oregon, Eugene, 1968.

DYER, H. S., "Toward Objective Criteria of Professional Accountability in the Schools of New York City," *Phi Delta Kappan*, LII, No. 4 (December, 1970).

EASTMOND, J. N., *Need Assessment: Winnowing Expressed Concerns for Critical Needs*. Salt Lake City, Utah: World-Wide Education and Research Institute, April, 1969.

EDUCATIONAL TESTING SERVICE, "Highlights of a Report from Educational Testing Service to the State Board of Education of The Commonwealth of Pennsylvania: A Plan for Evaluating the Quality of Educational Programs in Pennsylvania." Princeton, N. J., June 30, 1965.

ENGLISH, F. W., "Change Strategies That Fail," *California School Boards*, May, 1969.

ERIKSON, B., "A Systems Approach to Educational Technology (with Special Reference to Swedish Conditions)," *Educational Technology*, June, 1969.

ETZIONI, A., *Modern Organizations*, Foundations of Modern Sociology Series, Englewood Cliffs, N.J.: Prentice-Hall, Inc., 1964.

FERGUSON, R. L., "Computer-Assisted Criterion-Referenced Testing." Learning Research and Development Center, University of Pittsburgh, Pittsburgh, Pa., March, 1970.

FINN, J. D., "Technology and the Instructional Process," *AV Communication Review*, VIII, No. 1 (Winter, 1960).

FISHER, G. H., "The Analytical Bases of Systems Analysis," in D. I. Cleland and W. R. King, *Systems, Organizations, Analysis, Management: A Book of Readings*. New York: McGraw-Hill Book Company, 1969.

FLANAGAN, JOHN C., "The Critical Incident Technique," *Psychological Bulletin*, LI, No. 4 (July, 1954).

——, "Individualizing Education," *Education*, XC, No. 3 (February–March, 1971).

FRANKL, V. L., *Man's Search for Meaning: An Introduction to Logotherapy*. Boston: Beacon Press, 1962.

——, *The Doctor and the Soul: from Psychotherapy to Logotherapy*, 2nd ed. New York: Alfred A. Knopf, 1965.

——, *Psychotherapy and Existentialism: Selected Papers on Logotherapy*. New York: Washington Square Press, 1967.

——, *The Will to Meaning: Foundations and Applications of Logotherapy*. New York: The World Publishing Company, 1969.

GAGNE, R. M. (Ed.), *Psychological Principles in System Development.* New York: Holt, Rinehart and Winston, Inc., 1962.

GALLUP, G., "Second Annual Survey of the Public's Attitude Toward the Public Schools," *Phi Delta Kappan*, October, 1970.

GERARD, R. W. (Ed.), *Computers and Education.* New York: McGraw-Hill Book Company, 1967.

GERLETTI, R. C., "Producing An ITV Program," *Educational Television*, June, 1969.

GIBSON, T. L., "Instructional Systems Design Through In-Service Education," *Audiovisual Instruction*, September, 1968.

GLASER, R., "Psychological Bases for Instructional Design," *AV Communication Review*, Winter, 1966.

————, and A. J. NITKO, *Measurement in Learning and Instruction.* Learning Research and Development Center, University of Pittsburgh, Pittsburgh, Pa., March, 1970.

HANSEN, D. N., "Current Research Development in Computer-Assisted Instruction," Project NR 154-280, Tech. Memo No. 17. Sponsored by Personnel and Training Research Programs, Psychological Sciences Division, Office of Naval Research, Washington, D.C., Florida State University, February 15, 1970.

HARMAN, W. W., "Nature of Our Changing Society: Implications for Schools." Part I of *Social and Technological Change: Implications for Education.* ERIC/CEA, University of Oregon, Eugene, 1970.

HARMON, P., "Curriculum Cost-Effectiveness Evaluation," *Audivisual Instruction*, XV, No. 1 (January, 1970).

HARSH, J. R., R. A. KAUFMAN, and L. E. SHUCK, "A Proposed Continuation Model for ESEA Title III Projects." Task Force 8, ESEA Title III Office, California State Department of Education, Sacramento, Calif., 1968.

HARTLEY, H. J., "Twelve Hurdles to Clear Before You Take on Systems Analysis," *American School Board Journal*, July, 1968.

————, "Limitations of Systems Analysis," *Phi Delta Kappan*, May, 1969.

HELPER, J. W., "Assessing Educational Outcomes in Colorado." Rept No. 2, Colorado Department of Education, Denver, Colo., December, 1970.

HITT, W. D., "Two Models of Man," *American Psychologist*, July, 1969.

HOBAN, C. F., "The Usable Residue of Educational Film Research," in *New Teaching Aids for the American Classroom*, W. Schramm ed. Institute for Communication Research, Stanford University, 1960. Reprinted by U.S. Department of Health, Education and Welfare, OE-34020, 1962.

HOLTZ, J. N., "An Analysis of Major Scheduling Techniques in the Defense Systems Environment," in D. I. Cleland, and W. R. King, *Systems, Organizations, Analysis, Management: A Book of Readings.* New York: McGraw-Hill Book Company, 1969.

JAMISON, COLLEEN, and JEANNE McLEOD-GUERTIN, "Two System Models for Educational Planning," *Educational Technology*, June, 1969.

JOHNSON, D. W., "A Look At the Future of California Education," *California School Boards*, September, 1968.

KANE, R. M., "A System Approach: Accountability with 'Justice.'" Presented to a Symposium on Instructional Systems, Eighth Annual Convention of the National Society for Programmed Instruction, Anaheim, Calif., May 2, 1970.

KATZENBACH, E. L., "Planning, Programming, Budgeting Systems: PPBS in Education." The New England School Development Council, March, 1968.

KAUFMAN, R. A., "The System Approach, Programmed Instruction and the Future." Paper presented to the New York University Thirty-Fifth Annual Junior High School Conference, May, 1962.

———, "A System Approach to Programming," in G. Ofiesh, and W. C. Meierhenry, *Trends in Programmed Instruction.* Washington, D.C.: National Society for Programmed Instruction and National Education Association Department of Audiovisual Instruction, 1964.

———, "A Preliminary Selected Bibliography of System Analysis and System Synthesis as it Relates to Education and Training," OPERATION PEP. San Mateo County (Calif.) Department of Education, December, 1967.

———, "A System Approach to Education: Derivation and Definition," *AV Communication Review*, Winter, 1968.

———, "An Educational Management System." Paper presented to the Third Annual Conference in Innovations in Educational Management, Nova University, Fort Lauderdale, Fla., April 14, 1969a.

———, "Toward Educational System Planning—Alice in Educationland," *Audiovisual Instruction*, May, 1969b.

———, "A System Approach," a multi-media presentation. Department of Audiovisual Extension, University of Minnesota, Minneapolis, 1970a.

———, "System Approaches to Education—Discussion and Attempted Integration, Part III of *Social and Technological Change: Implications for Education*, ERIC/CEA. University of Oregon, Eugene, 1970b.

———, "A Possible Integrative Model for the Systematic and Measurable Improvement of Education," *American Psychologist*, Vol. XXVI, No. 3 (March, 1971a).

———, "Accountability, A System Approach and the Quantitative Improvement of Education—An Attempted Integration," *Educational Technology*, Vol. XI, No. 1 (January, 1971b).

———, W. CLINKENBEARD, and R. WOOD, "A Generic Educational Planning Model." The Los Angeles County Supplementary Education Center, Los Angeles, Calif., May, 1969.

———, and R. E. CORRIGAN, "The Steps and Tools of System Analysis as Applied to Education," OPERATION PEP. San Mateo County (Calif.) Department of Education, December, 1967.

———, BETTY O. CORRIGAN, and D. L. GOODWIN, "Mission Analysis in Education," OPERATION PEP. San Mateo County (Calif.) Department of Education, December, 1967a.

———, "Functional Analysis in Education," OPERATION PEP. San Mateo County (Calif.) Department of Education, December, 1967b.

————, and S. L. LEVINE, "Task Analysis in Education," OPERATION PEP. San Mateo County (Calif.) Department of Education, December, 1967c.

————, R. E. CORRIGAN, and C. L. NUNNELLY, "The Instructional System Approach to Training," *Human Factors*, VIII, No. 2 (April, 1966).

————, M. J. RAND, F. ENGLISH, J. M. CONTE, and W. HAWKINS, "An Attempt to Put the Ten Objectives of Education Developed for Pennsylvania by Educational Testing Service Into Operational Definitions." Temple City, Calif., Unified School District, April, 1968.

————, R. E. CORRIGAN, and D. W. JOHNSON, "Toward Educational Responsiveness to Society's Needs—A Tentative Utility Model," *Journal of Socio-Economic Planning Sciences*, Vol. III (August, 1969).

————, and J. R. HARSH, "Determining Educational Needs—An Overview." California State Department of Education, Bureau of Elementary and Secondary Education, PLEDGE Conference, October, 1969.

KERSHAW, J. A., and R. N. McKEAN, "Systems Analysis and Education." RAND Corporation, Research Memorandum 2473-FF, October, 1959.

KOCHMAN, A. F., "Educational Applications of the System Analysis and System Synthesis Processes," System Development Corporation, Rept. SP-3365, May 28, 1969.

LANDRY, L., "Management by Objectives." Paper presented to Academy on Educational Engineering, Bowman's Lodge, Wemme, Oreg., August 11, 1970.

LASWELL, H. D., *The Communication of Ideas.* New York: Harper & Row, Publishers, 1948.

LEE, A. MAUGHAN, "Instructional Systems: Which One?" *Audiovisual Instruction*, XV, No. 1 (January, 1970).

LEHMANN, H., "The Systems Approach to Education," *Audiovisual Instruction*, February, 1968.

LESSINGER, L. M., *Every Kid A Winner.* New York: Simon & Schuster, 1970a.

————, "Engineering Accountability for Results into Public Education." Paper prepared for Educational Linkup Conference, Washington Hilton Hotel, Washington D.C., January 29, 1970b. (Sponsored by U.S. Office of Education and Aerospace Educational Foundation and E.S.70.)

————, "The Powerful Notion of Accountability in Education." Paper presented to Academy on Educational Engineering, Bowman's Lodge, Wemme, Oreg., August 10–14, 1970c.

————, "Introduction to Performance Contracting." Presented to Academy on Educational Engineering, Bowman's Lodge, Wemme, Oreg., August 10–14, 1970d.

————, "Improved School Management Capability: Response to Accountability." Paper presented to Academy on Educational Engineering, Bowman's Lodge, Wemme, Oreg., August 13, 1970e.

————, "Evaluation and Accountability in Educational Management—Robbing Dr. Peter to 'Pay Paul.' " Paper presented to Academy on Educational Engineering, Bowman's Lodge, Wemme, Oreg., August 13, 1970f.

————, "Engineering Accountability for Results in Public Education," *Phi Delta Kappan*, LII, No. 4 (December, 1970g).

LIEBERMAN, M., "An Overview of Accountability." *Phi Delta Kappan*, Vol. LII, No. 4, Dec. 1970.

LIPHAM, J. M., R. T. GREGG, D. N. McISSAC, and R. G. MORROW, "Wisconsin Educational Needs Assessment Study." Department of Public Instruction, Madison, Wis., June, 1969.

ARTHUR D. LITTLE, INC., "Educational Needs in Montana." Superintendent of Public Instruction, State of Montana, December, 1968.

LOPEZ, F. M., "Accountability in Education," *Phi Delta Kappan*, LII, No. 4 (December, 1970).

LYNN, L. E., JR., "Systems Analysis—Challenge to Military Management," in D. I. Cleland, and W. R. King, *Systems, Organizations, Analysis, Management: A Book of Readings*. New York: McGraw-Hill Book Company, 1969.

MACDONALD, R. H., "A Programmed Instructional Course in the Management Process and An Information System to Support Its Decision-Making Responsibility." Chapman College, Orange, Calif., January, 1969.

MAGER, R. F., *Setting Instructional Objectives*. Palo Alto, Calif.: Fearon Publishers, Inc., 1961.

———, *Developing Attitudes Toward Learning*. Palo Alto, Calif.: Fearon Publishers, Inc., 1968.

———, and K. M. BEACH, JR., *Developing Vocational Instruction*. Palo Alto, Calif.: Fearon Publishers, Inc., 1967.

MASLOW, A., *Toward a Psychology of Being*, 2nd ed. Princeton, N.J.: D. Van Nostrand Company, Inc., 1968.

MAUCH, J., "A Systems Analysis Approach to Education," *Phi Delta Kappan*, January, 1962.

MEALS, D., "Heuristic Models for Systems Planning," *Phi Delta Kappan*, January, 1967.

MICHIGAN DEPARTMENT OF EDUCATION, ESEA Title III, "A Study of Educational Needs," 1969.

MILLER, R. B., "A Method for Man–Machine Task Analysis." Wright Air Development Division, U.S. Air Force, American Institutes for Research, WADC Tech. Rept. 54–563, December, 1954.

MOOD, A. M., "Some Problems Inherent in the Development of a Systems Approach to Instruction." Paper prepared for the Conference on New Dimensions for Research in Educational Media Implied by the "Systems Approach to Instruction," Center for Instructional Communications, Syracuse University, April 2–4, 1964.

MORGAN, C. T., J. S. COOK, A. CHAPANIS, and M. W. LUND, *Human Engineering Guide to Equipment Design*. New York: McGraw-Hill Book Company, 1963.

MORRILL, C. S., "Setting Programmed Instruction Objectives Using A Systems Methodology," in G. Ofiesh, and W. C. Meierhenry, *Trends in Programmed Instruction*. Washington, D.C.: National Society for Programmed Instruction and National Education Association Department of Audiovisual Instruction. 1964.

MORRISON, E. J., "Defense Systems Management: The 375 Series," in D. I. Cleland and W. R. King, *Systems, Organizations, Analysis, Management: A Book of Readings.* New York: McGraw-Hill Book Company, 1969.

NADLER, G., "Systems Design and Systems Development." Paper presented to Academy on Educational Engineering, Bowman's Lodge, Wemme, Oreg., August 10, 1970.

NESS, A., DEBORAH FORSTER, E. KAIRLES, J. GEARY, and A. E. PAGLIARINI, "The Amelioration of Critical Educational Needs in Minnesota Through Innovative and Exemplary Programs." Minnesota State Department of Education, St. Paul, June, 1969.

OFFICE OF EDUCATION, (DEPARTMENT OF HEALTH, EDUCATION, AND WELFARE), Educational Linkup Conference, *Proceedings*, Washington, D.C.: Washington Hilton Hotel, January 29, 1970.

OFIESH, G. D., *Programmed Instruction: A Guide for Management.* New York: American Management Association, 1965.

————, and W. C. MEIERHENRY, (eds.), *Trends in Programmed Instruction.* National Association for Programmed Instruction and National Education Association Department of Audiovisual Instruction, Washington, D.C., 1964.

OLSON, A. R., "Colorado People and Colorado Education—An Assessment of Educational Needs Based on the Population, Economy, and Social Structure of Colorado." Colorado Department of Education, Denver, June, 1970.

O'TOOLE J. F., JR., "Systems Analysis and Decision-Making in Education." SP-2020/000/01, System Development Corporation, Santa Monica, Calif., June 28, 1965.

PARKER, S., "PPBS," *California Teachers Association Journal*, May, 1969.

PARNELL, D., "To Achieve Significant Improvements in Education, State Government Must Take the Lead in Systematic Planning and Evaluation." Paper presented to Academy on Educational Engineering, Bowman's Lodge, Wemme, Oreg., August 10, 1970

PENNSYLVANIA DEPARTMENT OF PUBLIC INSTRUCTION, "A Summary Statement of Assessment of Educational Needs in The Commonwealth of Pennsylvania in Response to Section 305 (b) (1) of P. L. 90–247—ESEA Title III." Department of Public Instruction, Harrisburg, Pa., 1969.

PIELE, P. K., T. L. EIDELL, and S. C. SMITH, Eds. *Social and Technological Change: Implications for Education*, ERIC/CEA. University of Oregon, Eugene, 1970.

PIEPER, W. J., J. D. FOLLEY, JR., A. P. CHENZOFF, and H. H. VALVERDE, "Learner-Centered Instruction (LCI)," Vol. III—*Plan of Instruction*. AMRL-TR-116, Aerospace Medical Research Laboratories, Aerospace Medical Division, Air Force Systems Command, Wright-Patterson Air Force Base, Ohio, October, 1968.

POPHAM, W. J., *Educational Objectives*. Los Angeles, Calif.: Vimcet Associates, 1966.

————, *Selecting Appropriate Educational Objectives*. Los Angeles, Calif.: Vimcet Associates, 1967.

————, "Probing the Validity of Arguments Against Behavioral Goals." A presentation made to The American Educational Research Association, Chicago, February, 1968.

PORTER, E. H., "The System Thinker: Parables and Paradigm." System Development Corporation, SP-285, 1961.

QUADE, E. S., "Systems Analysis Techniques for Planning-Programming-Budgeting," in D. I. Cleland and W. R. King, *Systems, Organizations, Analysis, Management: A Book of Readings*. New York: McGraw-Hill Book Company, 1969.

RAND, M. J., "Effective Use of Personnel and Compensation Plans in Educational Management." Paper presented to Academy on Educational Engineering, Bowman's Lodge, Wemme, Oreg., August 12, 1970.

RANDALL, R. S., "An Operational Application of the CIPP Model for Evaluation," *Educational Technology*, IX, No. 7 (July, 1969).

RAPOPORT, A., forward to *"Modern Systems Research for the Behavioral Scientist*, W. Buckley, Ed. Chicago: Aldine Publishing Company, 1968.

RATH, G. J., "PPBS is More Than A Budget: It's A Total Planning Process," *Nation's Schools*, Vol. LXXXII (November, 1968).

ROGERS, C., "Toward a Modern Approach to Values: The Valuing Process in the Mature Person," *The Journal of Abnormal and Social Psychology*, LXVIII, No. 2 (1964).

ROGERS, E. M., "Developing A Strategy for Planned Change." Paper presented at the Symposium on the Application of System Analysis and Management Techniques to Educational Planning in California, OPERATION PEP, Chapman College, Orange, Calif., June, 1967.

————, *Diffusion of Innovations*. Glencoe, Ill.: The Free Press of Glencoe, 1962.

RUCKER, W. R., "A Value-Oriented Framework for Education and the Behavioral Sciences," *The Journal of Value Inquiry*, III, No. 4 (Winter, 1969).

————, V. C. ARNSPIGER, and A. J. BRODBECK, *Human Values in Education*. Dubuque, Iowa: William C. Brown Book Company, 1969.

RYAN, T. ANTOINETTE, "Systems Techniques for Programs of Counseling and Counselor Education," *Educational Technology*, June, 1969.

SAN FRANCISCO UNIFIED SCHOOL DISTRICT SUPPLEMENTARY EDUCATIONAL CENTER, ESEA Title III, "Needs Assessment. Phase I: Preliminary Overview," 1968.

SCHWITZGEBEL, R. L., "Behavior Instrumentation and Social Technology," XXV, *American Psychologist*, No. 6 (June, 1970).

SCIENTIFIC EDUCATIONAL SYSTEMS, INC., "Joint Federal State Task Force on Evaluation—Comprehensive Evaluation System Current Status and Development Requirements," Prepared for the joint State/Federal Task Force on Evaluation, January 8, 1970.

SHANNON, C. E., and W. WEAVER, *The Mathematical Theory of Communication.* Urbana: University of Illinois Press, 1949.

SHUCK, L. E., "The Instructional Tasks Project," Newport-Mesa Unified School District (California), 1968.

SILVERN, L. C., "Cybernetics and Education K–12," *Audiovisual Instruction*, March, 1968.

———, "Introduction" (Special issue, "Applying Systems Engineering Techniques to Education and Training"), *Educational Technology*, June, 1969a.

———, "LOGOS: A System Language for Flowchart Modeling," *Educational Technology*, June, 1969b.

SMART, J. M., and W. B. SPALDING, "Concepts of System and Higher Education," *The Educational Forum*, XXXIV, No. 2 (January, 1970).

SMITH, R. G., "The Development of Training Objectives." The George Washington University Human Resources Research Office Bull. 11, June, 1964.

———, "The Design of Instruction Systems." The George Washington University Human Resources Research Office, TR 66–18, November, 1966.

STATE UNIVERSITY OF IOWA AND NEA DEPARTMENT OF AUDIO-VISUAL INSTRUCTION, "Summary Report of the Second Lake Okoboji Audio-Visual Leadership Conference." Conference held at Iowa Lakeside Laboratory, Lake Okoboji, Milford, Iowa, August 19–22, 1956.

STEVENS, S. S., "Mathematics, Measurement and Psychophysics," in Stevens, *Handbook of Experimental Psychology*, New York: John Wiley & Sons, 1951.

STOLUROW, L. M., "Some Educational Problems and Prospects of a Systems Approach to Instruction." University of Illinois, Urbana, Tr No. 2 Training Research Laboratory, March, 1964.

STUFFLEBEAM, D. L., "Toward a Science of Educational Evaluation," *Educational Technology*, VIII, No. 14 (July, 1968).

SWEIGERT, R. L., JR., "Federal Aid: Placebo or Cure?" California State Department of Education, Department of Instructional Program Planning and Development, Sacramento, Calif., undated.

———, "Needs Assessment—The First Step Toward Deliberate Rather Than Impulsive Response to Problems. How to Do It." California State Department of Education. Paper presented at a conference of the Interstate Project for State Planning and Program Consolidation, U. S. Office of Education, San Francisco, Calif., April, 1968.

———, "The First Step in Educational Problem-Solving—A Systematic Assessment of Student Benefit, California State Department of Education, Bureau of Elementary and Secondary Education, PLEDGE Conference, October, 1969.

———, "Assessing Educational Needs to Achieve Relevancy," *Education*, XCI, No. 4 (April–May, 1971).

———, and D. KASE, "Assessing Educational Needs in California." Paper presented for the Region III Conference on Title III of ESEA, Denver, Col., March, 1969.

TANNER, C. K., "Techniques and Application of Educational Systems Analysis," *Audiovisual Instruction*, March, 1969.

THORESEN, C. E., "The Systems Approach and Counselor Education: Basic Features and Implications," *Counselor Education and Supervision*, IX, No. 1 (Fall, 1969), 3–17.

TOFFLER, A., *Future Shock*. New York: Random House, 1970.

TRZEBIATOWSKI, G. L., "An Evaluation of the Instructional Systems Approach in Higher Education." Doctoral thesis, Michigan State University, 1967.

TUCKER, J. A., "A Systems Approach to Effective Performance," in G. Ofiesh, *Programmed Instruction: A Guide for Management*. New York: American Management Association, 1965.

U. S. AIR FORCE SYSTEM COMMAND, *System Engineering*. Manual 375–5, 1965.

———, *Work Statement Preparation*, Manual 70–5, February 1, 1968.

U. S. DEPARTMENT OF DEFENSE, "Performance Measurement for Selected Acquisitions," DOD Instruction 7000.2, December 12, 1967.

U. S. GOVERNMENT, Mil. Standard 881—"Work Break Down Structure for Defense Material Items," November 1, 1968.

UTAH STATE BOARD OF EDUCATION, EDUCATIONAL PLANNING UNIT, "Educational Concerns," harvested from the Divisions in Utah's State Education Agency. Salt Lake City, Utah: April, 1969a.

———, Educational Planning Unit, "Educational Concerns: A Pilot Study for Harvesting Citizen Concerns Regarding Education." Salt Lake City, Utah: April, 1969b.

———, Educational Planning Unit, "Educational Concerns Implied by Base Data About the Future of Education." Salt Lake City, Utah: April, 1969c.

———, Division of Research and Innovation, "Critical Educational Needs in Utah's Public Schools." Office of the State Superintendent of Public Instruction. Salt Lake City, Utah: September 1, 1969d.

———, Concerns Analysis Task Force and the Educational Planning Unit, "A Report on the 1969 Needs Assessment Study of Utah Education." Salt Lake City, Utah: September, 1969e.

VALVERDE, H. H. and ELEANOR J. YOUNGS, *Annotated Bibliography of the Training Research Division Reports (1950–1969)*. Air Force Human Resources Laboratory, Air Force Systems Command, Brooks AFB, Texas, AFHRL–TR–69–11, September, 1969.

VANDERMEER, A. W., "Systems Analysis and Media—A Perspective," *AV Communication Review*, XII, No. 3 (Fall, 1964).

VON BERTALANFFY, L., "General System Theory—A Critical Review," in W. Buckley, (Ed.), *Modern Systems Theory for the Behavioral Scientist*. Chicago: Aldine Publishing Company, 1968.

WEAVER, W. T., "The Delphi Forecasting Method," *Phi Delta Kappan*, LII, No. 5 (January, 1971).

WEINER, N., "Cybernetics in History," in W. Buckley (ed.), *Modern Systems Research for the Behavioral Scientist*. Chicago: Aldine Publishing Company, 1968.

"What People Think About Their High Schools," The *Life* Poll by Louis Harris. *Life*, May 16, 1969.

White House Conference on Children, Report to the President, Washington, D.C., 1970.

WILDAVSKY, A., "A Program of Accountability for Elementary Schools," *Phi Delta Kappan*, LII, No. 4 (December, 1970).

index